PROVOKING

Uncommon Coaching for The Uncommon Soul

SUCCESS

Coach John S. Nagy, MSEM
Business and Life Coach

Provoking Success – Uncommon Coaching
for the Uncommon Soul

Copyright © 1989-2007 Coach John S. Nagy

Publisher: Promethean Genesis Publishing
PO Box 636
Lutz FL 33548-0636

ISBN-10: 0-9793070-0-7
ISBN-13: 978-0-9793070-0-3

First Printing, February 2007
Published in the United States of America
Book edited by Arthur Cornett and John S. Nagy

Book available at: www.provokingsuccess.com and
www.coach.net

The author is available for
speaking, workshop and coaching engagements.

Please contact him through his websites listed above
or by calling 813-949-0718

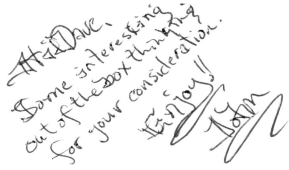

*Hi Dave,
Some interesting
out of the box thinking
for your consideration.
Enjoy!!
John*

To My Best Friend and Wife:

Candy – you inspire me to be far better then I could ever have imagined.

My Sons:

Steven and Jeffrey – you motivate me to improve what I offer and to deliver what I never dreamed I could.

My Best Buddies:

John "Jeff" Means and Arthur "Art" Cornett – your friendship, support, feedback and encouragement helped make this publication possible.

A couple of quick reference definitions and synonyms:

Provoke: translated verb [from the Latin: provocare, to challenge: from the root words: pro-, forth; and vocare, to call.]
- To call forth
- To provide the needed stimulus for
- To stir to action or feeling
- To incite to anger or resentment
- To give rise to; to evoke
- To bring about deliberately; to induce

Synonyms (Positive ones): *arouse, call forth, court, elicit, enkindle, evoke, excite, fire, foment, galvanize, get, incite, inflame, inspire, instigate, invite, kick up, kindle, motivate, move, pique, prod, prompt, propel, raise, ruffle, spur, stimulate, touch off, trigger, work up*

Other Synonyms (Whatever it takes!): *aggravate, anger, annoy, annoy continually or chronically, beset, bother, bug, burn (up), chafe, chevy, chivvy, chivy, disturb, enkindle, enrage, evoke, exasperate, fret, gall, galvanize, goad, harass, harry, hassle, impel, incense, inflame, infuriate, irk, irritate, madden, molest, nettle, peeve, plague, prick, rope, put out, rile, ruffle, set off, tempt, vex*

Success: translated noun [from the Latin successus, from past participle of succedere, to succeed.]
- Possessing continual and rightful creation of desired beneficial outcomes

Synonyms: *achievement, attainment, win, victory, triumph*

Antonym: *failure*

Coach's Note: *What does "provoking success" mean to you? More importantly, what will it mean to you after you have read this book? Come along and see!*

Table of Contents

Uncommon Introduction

Introductions set the tone for what you imagine is to follow.
Set it well and what follows will make perfect sense.
– Coach John S. Nagy

A. An Uncommon Upfront Request

Make the Most of This Book!

If you want to divide out the successful folks from all others, start sorting them by the actions they take while they are learning.
– Coach John S. Nagy

I challenge you to make the most bodacious use of this book by doing several things to maximize the return on your investment. Here they are:

1. *Purchase* a good pen, a highlighter pen & a blank notebook.

2. *Highlight* anything you read that makes sense, sparks insight for you or is usable in your business and in your life.

3. *Read only one chapter at a time* and *answer the following two questions* about each chapter **before** you proceed to the next chapter.

    a. *What did you get of value from reading this chapter and why is it valuable to you? Please respond fully to the question!* Use your notebook to record your responses. *Writing it down makes it "real."* This will give it a more bodacious impact in your life than what will occur by just thinking about it.

    b. Now that you have gotten something of value from reading this chapter, *how exactly do you plan to apply it in your business and in your life? Once again, please respond fully to the question!* Use your notebook to record your response. Make sure your plan is filled with *"result producing"* actions and that it has clearly defined time lines to act within to assure desired results.

4. Both respond to the questions and complete the action items in the *"Provoking Success!"* section at each chapter's end. *They are there for that purpose!*

5. *Review and use the notes and action plans* in your notebook on a regular basis to help *guide you toward accomplishing* that which your chapter questions provoke you to do.

6. If you have a coach, trainer, mentor, sponsor or trusted friend/partner, as you complete each chapter of this book,

    a. *share your responses with him or her*

    b. *discuss what you're getting from your reading*

    c. *have him or her help you refine your action plans*

    d. *empower him or her to help you hold yourself accountable for following through on your plans*

I structured this book to encourage you to complete one chapter each week. The chapters are grouped by general topic. They are not presented in a prescribed order so it doesn't matter which chapter you "take on" as long as you're working on one each week Taken one chapter per week, this book can be the basis of a year long project of transformation.

Once you've completed your year's journey through this book, I recommend that you repeat your "chapter a week" travel during the next year for an increased bodacious effect in your life. The chapters of this book intertwine and build on each other. As you gain greater insight and awareness from each chapter, *chapters you have previously read will take on a different feel and reveal more to your changing understanding if you should reread them.*

You also have an excellent opportunity to double and triple your return on your investment by *rereading this book and taking further action accordingly*. You'll thank yourself for doing so.

So, go ahead and be bodacious! Make the most of your investment and *provoke your success – now!*

Invest in your education by taking immediate action on what you've learned. – Coach John S. Nagy

B. An Uncommon Letter to You

Why Bodacious? – Coach John S. Nagy

Hello Reader!

Within the pages of this book, I hold a vision for you in the hope that your reading of this book will *provoke success* for you ***"bodaciously!"*** You may be asking yourself "Why 'Bodacious?'" and that's a great question to ask because it sets the tone for what is to follow.

Long before I ever understood its meaning or its significance to me, I loved the sound of the word "Bodacious." It possessed a strange energy within it that stirred my heart when I heard it. I've seen many definitions for "bodacious" over the years as I've come to know the word more intimately. Until I wrote this book, the two synonyms for "bodacious," that had stood out from the rest were "outstanding" and "remarkable." These definitions best represented what was captured in my heart whenever I used the word.

Now, years later, I understand "bodacious" as a possible way of being, the way how life should be and a label that is well earned by those who have embraced being bodacious for all the right... uh, "bodacious" reasons.

Here are some of those bodacious reasons for both using the word and living it:

<u>On a personal level,</u> being bodacious calls for being unrestrained by convention or propriety. It means not holding back the authentic self, even if it means breaking out of the original mold that can no longer contain it.

4

- *Is who we are now bigger then the mold that originally made us?*
- *Are we bodacious enough to show that we are bigger?*

<u>On a level that is foundational to our character or integrity,</u> being bodacious assures that whatever we do is noteworthy in every detail because this is a critical component of a worthwhile character. Our character is the mark we make in the book of life.

- *If what we do creates "a mark in the book of life," is that mark worthy of being made?*
- *Is our mark bodacious or is it just nonsense scribble?*

<u>On a social level,</u> being bodacious means that we are standing out and, more importantly, we are outstanding. It means more than just showing up and marking time. It means having an awesome (bodacious) overall influence on others that they appreciate and find attractive.

- *Are you bodacious with (and to) your friends and partners?*
- *Are they responding well to (and with) your bodacious nature?*

There's a neat rumor going around about this word "bodacious." You might have heard it. It's said that it came from a composite of "body" and "gracious." I like this connection. It's a strong indicator of how powerful this word is. When applied spiritually, being "bodacious" is "being a *continuous blessing* upon everyone you encounter."

- *If actions are not bodacious, they will manifest themselves as being common rather than grand.*
- *Are you bodacious?*
- *Look around and see what your world is telling – no, better yet – screaming at you!*

I believe that if you're not *being* bodacious, not *doing* things bodaciously, and not *manifesting* bodaciousness in the world – why bother at all?

Have a most awesome year!

Most bodaciously yours,

Coach John

PS - Am I being bodacious in writing this book and sharing it with you? Gosh, I hope so!

Be Bodacious! – Coach John S. Nagy

C. An Uncommon Lesson on Lessons

Every lesson presents itself until learned.
– Coach John S. Nagy

The Pacman video game mimics life's learning lessons. If you
don't see how, you're missing a vital connection to growth.
Much like any good educational tool, Pacman is simple in
construct and principle, and powerful in its ability to improve
skills and agility.

- ☑ The demands on the student present themselves quickly
- ☑ The results of choices deliver just as quickly
- ☑ Choice and consequence bind tightly together with little
  delay in delivery
- ☑ The reward for pattern recognition occurs through a variety
  of means
- ☑ Mastery of noise (and other distractions) filtering occurs
- ☑ Anticipatory reflexes and choice prioritization develop
- ☑ Mastery of the current level is required to advance to higher
  levels
- ☑ Advancement means more excitement and fun
- ☑ Abilities and beliefs are challenged for all the right reasons

Pacman is truly a microcosm of effective learning. Are you
starting to see the connection to life's learning lesson's yet?

Let's describe the mimicry in more detail. To play Pacman:

- ☑ You have a path you must go through completely.
- ☑ You must leave no path untouched until you achieve
  specific goals.
- ☑ You must accomplish certain tasks that empower you to
  perform more successfully at the next level.
- ☑ You must avoid specific unpleasantness that would
  diminish you and eventually remove you from the game.

☑ You must learn to navigate skillfully through the paths presented to earn the right to go to the next level.
☑ Each new level presents new challenges to be mastered.
☑ You proceed to higher levels once the lessons of the current level are learned.
☑ You learn to accept that the pattern of the game continues to repeat itself.

Like life, the details of this pattern allow you to learn quickly *even when things don't go well.*

If you fail at one level due to a series of bad choices, lack of skill, or not quickly anticipating undesired situations, the game requires you to start over at the lowest level. The fortunate thing about this is, since you've already mastered the lower levels you can quickly go through them and rise back to the level that's currently challenging you. The lower level skills have already become so ingrained in your playing patterns that you merely replay the level, suffer no setbacks or penalties, and get back to the level where you previously failed.

If you've played Pacman before, you could say that playing on one of these lower levels doesn't require much thought. You "just do it" because the levels facing you don't require your full concentration. You have already acquired the skills to know:

☑ what things to look for and what things to avoid
☑ what choices you need to make
☑ what skills you need to use
☑ what things to anticipate next
☑ some idea of what that next level looks like

Because you've been through this before, you know what you must do, and you execute the process flawlessly.

As your skill levels improve, you find that the investments (of time, energy, money and spirit) you have to make in order to play are not as costly as your initial investments were. The return on your initial investments now allows you to play for a longer time, at higher levels, with more action, excitement, and challenge. You look forward with growing eagerness to engaging in the "play."

As time advances, you may even find yourself engaging with other players:

☑ You may compete to see how your skills compare with theirs. Your comparisons may include:
  o   how fast you can reach a specific level
  o   how many points you can score
  o   how high a level you can achieve
  o   any combination of these
☑ You may observe other players:
  o   to learn how they play
  o   when to take certain actions
  o   what to look for and what to look out for
☑ You may just want to watch:
  o   to enjoy
  o   to appreciate how well others have mastered the game

When you find an endeavor that is fulfilling for you, you may feel driven to share that experience with others.

Consider this, too: There is a dark side to this "game" which, like the lessons presented from our Pacman game, also mimics life's lessons. If you don't learn about this side of the game so you can learn to tell the difference, you will continue to make ever more investments of your time, your energy, your money, and your spirit into that dark side with very little to show in return.

Let's explore this "dark side" within a larger framework than that of a simple video game.

I think you'd agree that no sane person likes wasted action. No one deliberately says, "Hey, give me something that wastes my time, gives me more debt and leaves a big empty spot in my gut." Wasted effort leaves a person feeling frustrated and empty – this is not what anyone would ask for willingly. What's more, wasted action sets the stage for anger in all its forms – agitation, disappointment, irritability, depression and apathy. The ultimate consequence of wasted effort, for most people, is a growing unwillingness to take further action to invest in their lives. Futile action sucks the wind out of people's sails, takes away initiative, and leaves people feeling empty.

People *want* success – would you not agree? They want to have better control over what occurs in their lives. They want to know that what they're doing makes a worthwhile difference and anything that doesn't help you in *"**Provoking Success**"* in your life is part of this dark side.

I would bet that *you're* like most people in this respect. You want to assure that your actions – your investments of time, energy, money and spirit – are going to give you a better life and a feeling of fulfillment. I'd bet, too, that you'd probably welcome any insights about making this occur. It would be safe to say that you're not alone in your desires.

Like our Pacman game, insights into successfully facing the challenges of business and life come from a variety of sources. Some insights come through introspection – an internal look into one's personal life experiences and into the lessons one learns from those experiences that are now available to us for dealing with our present challenges. Other insights come externally, for example: from seminars (live or recorded), books, or friends and family, especially people whose experience we trust.

As I mentioned earlier in my Pacman analogy, we join or engage with others in order to compete, to learn, or simply to enjoy. I invite you to join with me, for all these reasons, in a book that will:

- ☑ Challenge your current thinking
- ☑ Present dynamic lessons
- ☑ Tickle your funny bone with (I hope!) subtle wit and warming wisdom

Above all, I want to give you an opportunity to understand more fully the "games" of life and of business while showing you how to "play" them for maximum benefit every day.

My *purpose* as a coach *is to help my clients transform their lives*; I trust that the coaching I offer through this book will "provoke" you to ever-greater success by preparing you to better meet the challenges of *your next level.*

"When a lesson keeps hitting you in the nose, you have yet to learn it. True learning changes behavior for the better."
– Coach John S. Nagy

Uncommon Thoughts

Ordinary thinking never gives extraordinary results.
— Coach John S. Nagy

1. Knowledge is NOT Power!

Knowledge is merely inventory – perhaps potential power at best.
– Coach John S. Nagy

All those commercials, "edutainment" shows and "infomercial" programs you've seen and heard for years have duped people into believing that "knowledge is power." Of course they won't tell you that, in reality, this statement is misleading, because to do so might very well put them out of business!

Therefore, they play a game with you: They present a "hook" designed to grab your attention – the cue is "invest in our direction and you'll be empowered." You buy the hook and invest your money and your time in the misconception. Sure, you get serviced. What occurs afterward though is that you continue with *business as usual*. Nothing changes; no empowerment takes place. The only thing that's different is that now you have more inventory on your bookshelf (and possibly in the recesses of your mind), less cash in your pocket, and they have more in theirs.

Most people (even many of those who play it) don't realize it's a game. If you're among those who haven't realized this yet, it may be costing you a pretty buck and some of your precious time, as well. This is something you probably cannot afford.

So, let's start our own game. It's called "the en-knowledgement" game. It begins with understanding the importance of truth in advertising. Here's the first truth:

> ***"All the information you're about to read in this book is absolutely useless unless you take action on it."***

There, I said it: My disclaimer to the world is that the information contained in this book, by itself, will not make you powerful in any way – *unless you apply it in your everyday behavior.*

So, are you ready to get *en-knowledged*? Great!

Here's some background: Knowledge is a form of information analogous to muscle bulk in body builders. If you look at body builders, you see people who have invested time and effort to build their muscles. This investment is displayed quite prominently in their bodies.

If you asked them, most people would probably say, "Body builders are strong." They might also say, "Body builders are powerful." It might surprise you that these statements are not synonymous. The first statement only means that the body builder has (an inventory of) well-developed muscles. The second statement is only a projection of what the observer has in mind that body builders can potentially do with all that brawn. That's the key to this whole picture: What shows a body builder to be *powerful* is what they *do* with that inventory. If that body builder takes a single muscle relaxant, then that prime physical specimen has absolutely no power to *do* any action with all those muscles. The body builder can't draw from those muscles to take any action because the pathways between brain and brawn to cause action have been blocked.

Here's a helpful way to remember this: Think of *knowledge equating to inventory* and *power equating to action & application* of that inventory. Business and life endeavors consist of a delicate balance *between taking action to build one's inventory* and *taking action to draw from that inventory to make a valuable difference in one's business or in one's life.*

This works the same way that body builders build their muscles.

They take actions to build their bodies and eventually have sufficient inventory (strength) to draw on to take further actions.

In business and in life, having more inventory (potential resources to draw on) allows for more resource choices. Of course, having too much inventory or not using the resources already on hand means a "stipation" (from "con·stipation" meaning "with·backlog") has occurred in the business and life flow. Things come to a halt very quickly when "stipation" occurs. *Flow* is action or potential that is being applied. When properly channeled, flow brings powerful results and potentially more inventory, such as money, time and energy resources.

These same principles apply to knowledge. It's important to continue to educate yourself. It's just as important to commit yourself to taking action on that knowledge once you've got it packed between your ears.

There are many times I've seen clients purchase training tapes and self-help books, flip through them or quickly view them, then place them on a shelf where they end up collecting dust. They received the *knowledge* part and to prove it they can point to the shelf holding their purchase. Has anything changed inside them, though? Has anything occurred – other than the exchange of currency for a product? Have they been empowered in any way? Most of the time, you'll find the answers to these questions are "no, no and no."

Next time you hear the drumbeaters thumping the "knowledge is power" rhythm, join with me in a silent smirk and know that we are not buying into their game. If the knowledge they offer can be *applied* immediately and make a *valuable, identifiable* difference for you, your business, and your life then go for it! If not, provoke yourself in another direction. Value your resources and don't waste them on things that make no difference for you. *Accruing useless stuff "stipates" and dis-empowers you.*

Provoking Success! (Coach's Review, Recommendations, Questions and Unreasonable Requests)

1. Knowledge is inventory; application of knowledge is power.
2. Do what knowledge asks us to do – take action. Apply it and make a difference.
3. Next time you're tempted to buy another "knowledge is power" resource, ask yourself, "How will I apply that information in my life? Be clear on your answer *before* you buy it.
4. If the applied knowledge makes no identifiable difference in your life, forget it and go on in a different direction.
5. What knowledge do you currently hold in great esteem that you have yet to apply? Make a list!
6. What's must occur for you to start applying it? Write out these conditions.
7. **Action Item:** Create an action plan to provoke these conditions into your life. Create a schedule and include any support that would assist your efforts.

Power requires both potential and flow; without either, you remain powerless. – Coach John S. Nagy

2. The Heart of Your Selections

A whole host of supportive decisions follows most good choices.
– Coach John S. Nagy

There's a world of difference between a person taking action based on choice and a person taking action based on decision. Many people might think that there are no differences between the two. If you're one of them, be open to thinking differently about this. The concepts wrapped around the differences are simple yet somewhat difficult to grasp if you've never given it much thought. Grasping them though can save you much time, energy and even heartache.

The core of any selection you make hinges on whether the influences driving that selection are coming from an internal driver or an external driver. True, most everything comes down to a subjective world and neither choice nor decision will escape from this reality. The important issue to remember is "how" your selection is swayed. Knowing this makes for far better selections then those made in the dark.

The influence that occurs with *"choice"* is reflected in the very root of the word. It means "taste" and it is akin to the word "gust" (as in "gusto" and "disgust"). When you make a choice, you make a selection based on your internal tastes. The ramifications of making selections based on "taste" are that you evaluate "what is before you" *based on what you want. This is personal and is internally driven.* Although there might be other selections available, the focus is not on what one will not experience, it is on *what one will experience as a result of the selection.*

Much like "choice," the influence that occurs with *"decision"* is reflected in its root too. It means "off-cut" or "to cut off" and is akin to separating that which you want from that which must be left behind, lost or dismissed. When you make a decision, there's always more then one selection on the table to consider. Although the selection may have some internal influences, the main issue that is up for consideration is the consequences one must face for opting for one selection versus others. In other words, *you're making a selection based on what you don't want.* By deciding, you get rid of that which you do not want – moving non -selected items external to your wanted situation.

Let's look at an example: You've chosen to get involved in a relationship where you're facing with many decisions. Some decisions involve how you will invest your time because there so many possibilities and it's not possible to fit them all in. Other decisions you need to make relate to which friends you will and won't be investing time with because there's just not enough time to include everyone. Still more decisions require you to consider which things to do and not do because – once again – time won't allow for all of them. Your initial choice was based on an internal desire to participate in a "relationship." This choice required many decisions that support keeping you involved in that relationship. These decisions opened up more possibilities for you than you originally envisioned or that you can realistically do. As a result, you have gained because of your initial choice and you have had to make selections to the exclusion of others.

The difficulty most people face in making decisions is that most people *want it all!* This presents a problem that sometimes cascades into other problems. If you're unwilling to let go and face loss due to options going away, you wind up with a situation in which you'll be stuck. This bind leads to indecision and often causes more pain than making the decision to begin with. People who have a tough time accepting or dealing with change are prime candidates for indecision.

18

All this being said, when it comes to making a choice or a decision, neither one nor the other is superior. Neither one will out shine the other if you continually make selections based on one rather than the other. What makes your selections superior is your conscious application of the two. That is the key to making superior selections – *knowing whether you are making a choice or a decision.*

Coach's Note: If you find yourself stuck, focus on what you truly want in the moment or better yet, what you want long term (which is a far better strategy). Make a choice. By doing so, you focus on what you most desire. When you do, what you might lose in relation to what you will gain often moves any obstacles out of your path. Please keep in mind that t*he demands of indecision often create more problems than the demands of the actual decision itself. Provoke action – make your selection!*

Provoking Success! (Coach's Review, Recommendations, Questions and Unreasonable Requests)

1. Create a list of situations where you know you have delayed making a selection or taking action.
2. Rate each situation on a scale from 1-10 with one being more of a choice and ten being more of a decision.
3. In clear terms, write down the personal or professional cost (time, money, energy spirit) of each delay or non-action.
4. In clear terms, write down what each situation tells you about what you want and what you don't want.
5. Write out the lessons that each situation presents to you.
6. **Action Item:** Based on the lessons presented, what can you do different next time similar situations come up?

Self-knowledge is important! If you know what you truly want, decisions become much easier. – Coach John S. Nagy

3. Efficiently and Effectively Frustrated

Effectiveness is founded on knowing the correct wall to lean your ladder. – Coach John S. Nagy

Here's a secret I share with you that may save you much heartache. It's about something you can do to improve your investment returns in business and in life. If you choose to make this investment, your returns will fare better than they would if you didn't. It has to do with understanding the distinction between "Efficiently" and "Effectively." Knowing, planning and acting on the differences will create much greater value for you and possibly others.

Let me start you down a more enriching road with very quick examples that will help your understanding. When I talk to folks about improving the bottom line in their business I often hear, "I just need to be more efficient in what I do, that'll make the difference" or "Efficiency is what I pride myself on and when I can make this more efficient, things will really take off!" In the meantime, I'll be getting all sorts of other messages and indications that what they truly want is not what they're getting – no matter how hard they are trying.

This is very understandable. Not getting what you truly want breeds frustration and many of us have that! If you're wondering what that frustrated emotional energy is telling you, try on this old saying: "Keep doing what you've always done and you'll always get what you've always gotten." Do you see the connection?

The message of "frustration" is "You are taking futile action!" and it's amazing how some of us don't get this simple message. Trying harder will not change the results in these situations. The actions taken are not effective. As you might suspect, entrenched

20

beliefs die-hard and the "efficiency" belief is one of them. For those of you not familiar with it, here it is:

- ***Common Misnomer: "The Efficiency Belief"*** - *Efficiency is the key to success. To maximize the Return on Investment (ROI) one must assure that there is no waste in the use of resources in doing something. Hence to "win" at the game and get the biggest bang for one's buck, one must assure that the activities are streamlined, taking no unnecessary actions and using no unnecessary resources to accomplish the task(s) at hand.*

Many people hold this belief, especially in the technical professions – ever hear of the 1960's "Efficiency Expert"? Embarrassingly enough, I invested in this belief myself in the past. Since then, I've been graced with the following tidbit of information: Belief in "efficiency" needs to be balanced first with belief in "effectiveness." To give you an idea of how this concept works, let's ponder the following statements:

- *Efficiency* is doing things right. *Effectiveness* is doing right things.
- *Efficiency* is a management function. *Effectiveness* is a leadership function.
- *Efficiency* focuses on "method." *Effectiveness* focuses on "purpose."

Notice what's really going on here. You could have the most efficient operation on earth; yet never really get what you want if what you're efficient at doesn't serve your true purpose.

Here's an example to illustrate this point: It may be very "efficient" not to use the shift key while typing – placing the "Caps lock" key either totally off OR TOTALLY ON MAKES IT MORE EFFICIENT TO TYPE – BUT THE EFFECT THIS "EFFICIENCY" CHOICE HAS ON THE READER IS

PROBABLY NEITHER THE ONE THAT IS EXPECTED NOR DESIRED.

(Have you ever run into someone who communicates like this? Is it more efficient for you to read something written efficiently like the example above? What is the effect on the reader? Is it efficient?)

Here's another example: A sloth is a very "efficient" user of energy. However, would you like your operations – your day-to-day dealings – to have a sloth's metabolism in our speedy economy?

Next time you're looking to improve your business, ask yourself about the "effectiveness" of your operations and focus instead on your purpose. Once you've assured yourself that your purpose is being served, that you're "doing right things," then you can go back to "doing things right."

One more example of this is in the use of a ladder. You can:

- work at being the best ladder climber in the world
- have your ability to climb the ladder honed so well that it takes you very little effort and resource to make it to the top – an earmark of efficiency
- win great acclaim for being the most efficient ladder climber ever

People might even say that you are very effective at climbing ladders – if climbing ladders is the goal – and they would be right. Most people fixated on efficiency only see the climb that is involved and feel delight when recognized for it.

If you step back from the situation, you may realize that the main goal of climbing a ladder is not to climb it. Climbing is only an action that supports a higher purpose. The ladders' true function is to *reach a place purposefully*. To accomplish this, you must have the ladder purposely positioned to take advantage of each climb. If you fixate on efficiency, you'll believe the purpose of ladder climbing is to be the best in that function. If you focus on effectiveness, you know your purpose is to have the ladder properly positioned to take advantage of the climb. You know you must have that *effect*, before you can *benefit* from climbing the ladder. People focusing on effectiveness feel delight when the advantage of the climb is accomplished. Your goal should be to focus on the effect you want, *then* on the efficiency.

To keep the two working in harmony you merely need to focus on the benefits! The benefit of efficiency is maximum return for minimum investment. The benefit of effectiveness is you get what you planned on getting – which requires a purposeful focus other then just being efficient.

When you're truly acting on your purpose, you provoke the extra motivation you need to succeed even when frustration is at its max. Don't you deserve that extra energy? That's bodacious!

Provoking Success! (Coach's Review, Recommendations, Questions and Unreasonable Requests)

1. Efficiency and effectiveness are not synonymous.
2. Efficiency is doing things right. Effectiveness is doing right things.
3. Efficiency is a management function. Effectiveness is one of leadership.
4. Efficiency focuses on "method." Effectiveness focuses on "purpose."
5. **Action Item:** Make sure you're working toward the effect you want *before* you work on efficiency.

Climbing the wrong wall efficiently is ineffective.
– Coach John S. Nagy

4. Responsibly Accountable

Understanding the difference between 'responsibility' and 'accountability' is knowing what 'taking action' and 'facing outcome' is all about" – Coach John S. Nagy

I heard it again today and it tore at my insides. It was the old "I'm a responsible person" defensive war cry and it was coming from someone who was definitely not behaving responsibly.

What was so sad about this was that this person had no clue as to what they were really saying. They really *thought* they *were* being responsible. That's the sad part. They showed all the signs of irresponsibility with no awareness of it. Let me explain:

As a business owner, you can't afford to be unaware of what genuine responsibility looks like. To get a firm grip on it, let's contrast the word "responsibility" with the word "accountability."

When first introduced to the contrast between the two words, I was doing college graduate study back in the early 90's. Up to that point, I thought the two words were interchangeable. Indeed, our teachers used them interchangeably, even after they'd taught and emphasized the words' supposed distinctions. I couldn't rely on the dictionary to get clarity; it listed them as synonyms!

When we use the words "responsibility" and "accountability" interchangeably, we cause confusion. We also introduce fuzziness in the way we operate and in the systems we employ. To obtain clarity and have it affect our business in positive ways, we must understand that the two words focus on two entirely different aspects of our operations. Because they are so closely tied to each other, the confusion is understandable.

So, let's shake them out and get some clarity.

24

- **Responsibility** is about "doing." People "take on" responsibilities. Someone who takes responsibility for something takes action to do the task. This includes making decisions. Responsibility is agreed to "up front" or necessary tasks aren't done because no one was assigned to do it.

Problems with accepting responsibility are most evident in committee work when the leader forgets to assign tasks to members or asks who's going to do what. (Have you ever come out of a group meeting wondering who's supposed to take what action on all the great plans discussed?)

- **Accountability** is about reporting on "outcomes" and "results." It's also a willingness to "face the music" when all is said and done. Accountability is reporting on what you've gained—or lost – from the actions taken. Part of being accountable is standing by the results and answering for them, whether or not you "took on" the responsibility for the action itself. Anyone holding another person accountable for the results of actions and decisions has assigned accountability to that person – whether that person wanted to be held accountable or not. You see this every day in business operations. The workers – not the supervisor – are responsible for doing the work. Upper management will hold the supervisor accountable for the results – not the workers – since it was the supervisor's responsibility to choose the right workers to hold those responsibilities.

To have true "accountability," there must be an empowerment of one party by an authority through an agreement by both. The person accountable must be empowered by someone to authorize actions to take place with the power to make those actions occur. This assures that the responsible party *can* take action to accomplish a task. A person must be empowered in order to be held accountable for results or lack of results. Without empowerment, accountability doesn't have the desired impact and probably won't accomplish the desired actions.

If you want to know what empowerment is, without any confusion, merely substitute the word "authority." If you're truly responsible, you have all the authority you need to carry out the actions associated with that responsibility. With true authority comes the ability to take the actions necessary to complete the tasks. Of course, with true authority, the person responsible is usually the person held accountable since no one else was involved in the results produced by the actions that were taken.

In business systems, there are usually multiple divisions of tasks so there are usually limitations placed on any authority that is given. The resulting limited empowerment is understood to be enough to enable the completion of tasks. This limitation is often the source of many frustrations and even failures. To minimize this, business systems (and their designers – yes, that's you!) must make sure any responsibility given must have equivalent authority associated with it as part of that agreement.

Any kind of agreement without empowerment has no weight and so the system of interactions becomes a fruitless game. This is understandable. If a person is not going to be held accountable, they have no incentive to take or to cause action. There's no incentive for following through. The words, "Why bother?" will echo through the halls and all the plans that were made will fade along with that echo.

Here's an example to illustrate this point: When you hear a person claiming to be responsible, check to see if anything was *done,* since responsibility is "action based." They are not being responsible if they are not a "person of action." Another way to say this is that they are "unable" or "unwilling" to *respond with action.*

26

Here's one more example to "drive the point home": When you are dealing with a person who is unwilling to empower you (to give you authority), yet expects you to be accountable for outcomes, that person lacks the integrity you need from them in order to do further business with them. They are asking you to do the impossible!

To be held accountable, you must have some ability to affect the outcome. In this respect, to answer for any accountability, you must also have some responsibility associated with how things are to be handled – even if all you do is empower others to take action within some guidelines.

In this way, you would be held accountable if you chose the wrong people to do a job. Ultimately, the results, and the consequences, of your choices will fall in your lap if you were the one who had been empowered with the authority to make things occur, if, with all your efforts to get the right people for the job, you didn't achieve the outcome you expected.

This is why contracts are often used in business situations. They empower all parties *to do* and to create *beneficial outcomes* "all the bases are covered" and therefore, are beneficial to all the involved parties. When contracts are well written, they also provoke solutions to any default conditions that could occur.

Provoking Success! (Coach's Review, Recommendations, Questions and Unreasonable Requests)

1. **Action Item:** Take a quick assessment of yourself and others with whom you deal frequently. Are these individuals "people of effective action" or do they merely talk a good game? Do they continually make excuses for not having the results they promised? A good indication of this behavior is the use of the word "but" in any explanation, along with a finger pointing in some direction other than towards the person who is making the excuses.

2. Responsible people are "people of action" who deal with other "people of action." Always empower both parties to hold the other accountable for outcomes and results. (Does the phrase "the buck stops here" ring a bell?)

3. Accountability means you:
   a) Know in advance what you want as the outcome
   b) Are empowered – have authority – to affect outcomes.
   c) Create systems that assure accurate results reporting.
   d) Realize that there is always some responsibility associated with accountability – even if that responsibility is to delegate responsibility.
   e) Are willing to face and handle all queries regarding outcomes – no matter what.

4. **Action Item:** Ask yourself about situations in your own experience when you were asked to do something and you were not empowered to fully carry out the requested task. Were you able to get the requested results? What can you now do differently when you are not given authority that is equal to the responsibilities requested of you?

5. **Action Item:** Create a list and vision what you can do differently into the future. Plan and take action on it!

Effectiveness starts and ends with a willingness to take on responsibilities and accept accountability for outcomes.
– Coach John S. Nagy

5. Ditching the Positive Attitude

I once met a teacher who tried to be a good role model for his students by having a bad attitude toward his students' bad attitudes; he's still having attitude problems to this day.
— Coach John S. Nagy

Gosh, it would be so boring to read another "attitude is everything" story. Even worse would be trying to write one that people could actually pick up and read. Worse yet, the last thing I would ever want to do is try to convince others to "cop a positive attitude." I might however, try to convince *you* to ditch one if you happen to have one already.

You might say these are strong words coming from a business coach and personal developer. Let me share with you some of my thoughts and insights about positive attitudes: My experience is that most people have this idea that a positive attitude is a good thing and that most people benefit when they experience someone's positive attitude. As these same people practice "putting on" a positive mindset, they suffer disappointment when they realize that their supposedly positive attitude is not making their life, or the lives of others, any better.

There are elements that contribute to this. If you break down "what an attitude is" into its basic components, you'll see that being *"positive"* is not what most people think it's cracked up to be. That's because an attitude consists of four parts:

1. an *event* (followed by)
2. a *thought*, a conclusion or a belief (that generates)
3. *energy* (to take action – always emotion based) and
4. the *action* or behavior

When the results of the action (see above #4) are construed to be an event (see above #1) a continuous loop is created.

An example of this occurs in interactions between people: We encounter (#1 the event) a person who is naturally inclined toward smiling at others. We think, conclude, or believe (#2) they are being friendly toward us. Our belief gives us energy (#3) to move ourselves from whatever our previous mood was toward interest, enthusiasm, and joy. Our action or behavior (#4) is motivated by this energy. The resulting events (#1) are now viewed (#2) as friendliness toward this person. Should this person have an internal series of events (#1) similar to what we just had the situation would be amplified.

The cycle described above is re-enforced with a supporting cast of three characteristics:

1. how we choose to *perceive* the four components (of an attitude) as they occur
2. what kind of *value or importance* we place on them as they occur
3. what actions we *intend* to take as we invest ourselves in this process

The things I say here could sound like a bunch of nonsense until you put it all together. Once you choose to perceive "value" in *everything* that occurs (no matter what you've been trained to think in the past) then you start the process of creating a "valuing" attitude. I believe that a "valuing attitude" is a much deeper and richer attitude than that of the well-promoted "positive" one.

At this point, you might not see any difference between these two attitudes. I would agree with you if I had not experienced how differently people invest themselves into each of these two attitudes. The distinction between *positive* and *valuing* is subtle yet it is still important. Without understanding the meaning (the weight or *value)* we place on these words, the attitudes could be seen as being the same. They're not.

You could have a "positive" attitude about a thing or situation that has no actual value to you.

Here's an example to illustrate this point: Your partner comes to you with concerns regarding a situation. Your response attempts to redirect your partner's attention toward the improbability of the situation ever causing any major problems of any concern. In effect, your attempt to be positive actually discounts or has the effect of devaluing your partner's concerns. Your partner might appreciate that you were being "up beat" and projecting a positive attitude but it's more likely that his focus will be on how devalued and discounted he feels from your positive attitude.

If you do not show that you value your partner's ability to identify problems, any attempt to placate your partner with a positive attitude, as described above, will be viewed as discounting him. Because you place no value or importance on the concerns your partner expressed, your "positive" attitude toward your partner's view communicates your lack of support and how little your investment in your partner is. In other words, the surface of the water (your words) seems to be pleasant, but the undercurrent (of energy within you) is moving swiftly in another direction that holds more value and importance to you than your partner does.

Regardless of how well you show a "positive attitude" toward others, after a while, most people become aware of your deeper attitude – how little you truly value their situations and how much your values, energies, and interests are flowing as a hidden undercurrent in some other direction. Realizing this, they will invest themselves very slightly (or not at all) in matters where it is clearly obvious by your attitudes and behaviors that your values (your valuing attitude) are elsewhere – they will no longer trust or tolerate your "positive" message.

How ironic this is. Your positive attitude ends up putting off the very people you want to impress or support even if you created it with the best of intentions. In truth, it was really put forth to make you look good or supportive or to avoid making undesired waves. What was the result? They sensed your hypocrisy, your lack of integrity, and came to question your underlying sincerity. Your attitude is ultimately devaluing!

Here's another example to ponder: Your partner comes to you with concerns regarding a situation. Your response affirms your partner's ability to both see these problems and take action to address them. You respond further by asking how your partner wants to have you participate in addressing the situation. Although you have a serious look on your face, your partner senses that you are valuing his or her concerns. You're willing to invest further in him or her by offering to engaged in assisting in the situation. Your attitude is neither positive nor negative – it's valuing! *It shows you to be invested in your partner.*

Put yourself in the place of the partner in the above examples. Which attitude would you prefer to encounter? When a "valuing" attitude is on the surface, rather than being an unseen undercurrent, others perceive you as being a person who consistently assigns value and importance to the things that really are of value and importance to you. You have integrity. Every intention you have (remember our third supporting characteristic of an attitude?) contributes to the workings of your own life and therefore makes an impact on others too. The energy generated by your intentions brings about actions and events that are beneficial or educational to you and/or to others (depending on the investment you and/or others have made to your intentions). People who intentionally value create a belief system within themselves that is reinforced by others. These "others" in turn view these intentionally valuing people as being authentic and consistently trustworthy – even if they do not hold the same values themselves. These relationships with others tend to strengthen with time and their reality is never questioned because of the consistency and trustworthiness they see and value

Why might you want to shift from a positive attitude to a valuing attitude? Because, while a positive attitude might be perceived by others as a pleasant one that doesn't rock any boats, a valuing attitude does so much more to:

- encourage and invite trust from others
- position you to continuously receive valuable opportunities

Your valuing attitude provokes others toward knowing that no matter what might occur for them, you'll always perceive and honor them as being worthwhile.

Provoking Success! (Coach's Review, Recommendations, Questions and Unreasonable Requests)

1. Know how your present attitudes were built and what your attitudes say about you to others.
2. Use the supporting cast to assist in the shift: *perception*, *value* and *intent*.
3. Choose to create an attitude that makes a valuable difference for you and for those whom you care about most.
4. Be authentic in whatever you choose to build.
5. **Action Item:** When you don't like the results of your present attitude, *examine* the events, beliefs, energies, and actions that built it. Is your attitude authentic? (I.e. Do your attitudes support or hinder you in the most effective & efficient usage of your time, energy, & resources towards doing the things that matter most to you?)

A cornerstone of attitude – good or bad – is the value you place on what is before you. – Coach John S. Nagy

6. The Right to Complain

The ride you signed up for should not include complaints if you knew what you purchased. – Coach John S. Nagy

I felt vaguely uneasy the other day during a conversation with a client. Then I figured out why: Had it not been for previous conversations, relating to some choices he'd made months back, I might not have felt that uneasiness and I could have let his words stand unchallenged. As it was, the recurring theme of this conversation was too much to ignore and I went to work sharing this insight with him.

"I have something frightening to share with you," I said. I went on to tell him that there's a little-known organization in the world, which many people could benefit from knowing about. This organization is both secret and anonymous. In fact, it's so secret and anonymous that many of its own members don't even know that they are a member. That's what makes it so scary. Its existence is not even based on a conscious conspiracy.

Before I share with you the name of this organization (or why I'm telling you this story), I want to focus in on three of the most interesting traits of its members.

The first trait is what I just mentioned: unawareness of membership. It's rare to see anyone who knows that they're a part of this organization and much less admits to being a member. They're oblivious to their membership. Even when they are prompted to admit to being a member, their behavior rarely changes afterward.

The second trait about these people is that they continuously complain. I don't mean intermittently. I mean they'll go for any opportunity to bend an ear, even to the point of nausea for the poor soul who crosses their path.

The third trait could be considered humorous, if it weren't so sad. This third trait deals with the direction in which they choose to complain. More specifically, they choose to complain in ways that accomplish no difference whatsoever.

The forth and final trait is the most frightening of all. It deals with the poor souls who come into the lair of the complainer. Unbeknownst to these people, the complainers whom they encounter *don't really want solutions* to their complaints. They're so caught up in the act of complaining that they can't hear solutions. To do so would alter both their "life and business" style and their manner of being. This would be intolerable to them. They would lose their membership in the organization! Pity the person who tries to help them, for he or she will be continually drained, and to no purpose. Membership in this group includes those people who only appear to either want a solution or claim they have no solutions. They really just want to be heard and to be validated (something they can only truly do for themselves.) Because they do not directly say what they really want, the effect on any one they encounter is usually a negative one because their game is usually misunderstood.

Scary? You bet!

When you put all these traits into a package, call it a "human being," and let these humans loose on the world, the effect is like pouring dry bags of concrete into a filled swimming pool. The first effect is that things get really cloudy. The second effect is that things in the pool slow down and eventually stop. The last effect is that all the people in the pool get stuck if they don't get out quickly enough. It's not a pretty picture.

I've nicknamed this organization "BMW Anonymous." This is not a reference to the vehicle (although people who are part of this group often want a free ride). The name is more of an acronym for what you hear when you get within earshot to a

BMW member. I'll be polite about this and simply say the "MW" stands for "moaning" and "whining."

An interesting thing to note is that BMW's are best known for their subtle modes of contributing to other people's workloads often through upward or lateral delegation. This occurs when other people who hear these complaints take them seriously and attempt to do something about these complaints – most of the time this is not a wise move.

Another interesting thing to note is BMW's often make choices while being fully aware of the consequences of their selection, and shortly after, they begin complaining bitterly about the very thing for which they opted. Very scary!

My client didn't immediately see his connection to what I was telling him, even though he'd been complaining for months about the lack of support he'd been getting from his corporate office.

After much thought and several attempts on his part to move into a different business environment, he decided to stay at his current place of employment. At that time, I commented that his decision meant that he'd be experiencing the same unchanged circumstances. He'd have to come to terms with his circumstances if he wanted to function effectively into the future. He agreed or at least that's what I thought at the time.

Yet, once again, here I was, listening to his complaints. Nothing had changed. These were the very complaints I'd heard from him months back.

At this point, I told him very bluntly that he had no right to complain. He vigorously protested and said his organization should not run like this. He believed that the only way to change his situation was to complain. I repeated to him that he had not earned the right to complain. He paused a moment, his face quizzical, and then, just as bluntly, asked me, "Why not?"

I said the facts were clear. He had known the company operated as it did long before he got there and the inertia within systems meant that they would continue to exist and perform as they always had. He had a chance to get out and he decided to stay, fully aware of the limitations and snags within the system. He'd selected the system and was now complaining about it. The only thing he had the right to complain about was his decision, because that was the only thing over which he had control. A spark of understanding flickered in his eyes.

I welcomed him to BMW Anonymous and asked him if he wanted to resign from the organization. Thinking I was talking about his business, he said "no." He really did want to continue working there.

I asked him again if he wanted to resign and specifically referred to BMW Anonymous. That flicker of understanding quickly flared to a flame. He connected with my point and answered, "Yes." I said, "Great, then complain in a direction that makes a difference – complain to yourself! Focus on what you can change – again, yourself. Own your decisions!"

He agreed and I haven't heard him complain about his situation since. In fact, because he changed his attitude he took actions soon after to work more effectively, efficiently, and enjoyably within the system in which he'd decided to play. His effectiveness has become bodacious and as a result, *he provoked his own success!*

Provoking Success! (Coach's Review, Recommendations, Questions and Unreasonable Requests)

1. Recognize BMW Anonymous traits when they are present – even when they are within you.

2. **Action Item:** When others are BMW members, contribute to their ability to be more effective by encouraging them to direct their complaints more profitably; then detach from their complaints for your own good and theirs!

3. **Action Item:** When you are the BMW member, focus on the extent of your "sphere of influence." Create a list of that which you do have control over and that which you don't. Own your decisions and make a bodacious difference in your sphere – the only one that matters and that you have control over.

Coach's Note: The "B" in BMW stands for "Belly-aching." *I hope you didn't think otherwise.*

True ownership accepts (and owns) without reservation or complaint. – Coach John S. Nagy

7. Mildew Will Do

Bargain for less and you will surely get it – Coach John S. Nagy

When I'm in a classroom or seminar setting, I like to use story problems to amplify what I'm teaching. This is particularly true when the lesson relates to the discipline often required to accomplish or obtain what we truly want in an appropriate manner, both in our professional lives as well as in our personal lives. I've learned to ask this question: "If you really wanted natural, 'un-tampered with' grapes to eat and all you ever got were raisins, what would you do next?"

In one of my classes, the answers were especially illuminating. Some students responded that they would complain to the source that it was grapes they wanted and not raisins. Their rationale was that if you don't ask, it's less likely that you'll get what you really want. The philosophy of the squeaky wheel was in full swing with this bunch. They figured if they complained enough and in the right way, they would eventually receive the grapes. I didn't have the heart to tell them that the squeaky wheel often doesn't get oiled – it gets yanked out and replaced.

Another group within the class said that they would reject the raisins at once, since raisins were not what they wanted. They were willing to wait for the real thing – even if it meant that they would starve. It seemed strange to me that the action they planned to take would likely never bring them what they truly wanted. Planned starvation was not too appealing to me, yet they were pretty convincing in their argument.

Other students rationalized that raisins are only dehydrated grapes. They got creative and said they'd merely drop their raisins into a glass of water, wait until the water was soaked up and then eat the re-hydrated raisins. After all, the only difference was one of water and the difference wasn't that big. Their unwavering conviction in their plan convinced me that they were well on their way to settling for less and being okay with it. They were impressive.

As the talking continued, there were almost as many reactions, and suggestions to solve the challenge, as there were students. The discussion was quite interesting.

At one point, I decided to make the problem more urgent, so I put forth some new constraints:

1. There were no more grapes anywhere;
2. The only thing left were raisins;
3. The raisins would only last a year or so; and
4. The desire for a natural, "un-tampered with" grape was still alive and well.

With this new game afoot, some groups who had opted to complain or wait said they would now opt for the re-hydration idea as the way to satisfy their desires. A surprising majority of the class opted for this. They said they would drop the raisins into water, let them plump up, and then eat them without a second thought.

I asked the class if this would satisfy their desire for a natural, "un-tampered with" grape. Their response was "Well, no, but it's close enough. After all, life doesn't always give you what you want." I shuddered at the general acceptance of this comment. It surely explains why I see so many people accepting less in their lives.

An interesting thing happened during all of this. One bright student broke into the discussion and said that the proposed solution would not do at all. This student said that the "grape to raisin" dehydration process changed the grapes irreversibly and therefore re-hydrated raisins would, at best, be "tampered with"

40

grapes. "They are not really the desired "un-tampered with" grapes that would bring me satisfaction," he said.

I then asked the student if he had another solution. The response I got was thought provoking. The student suggested planting the raisins and watering them to help them germinate and grow. The obvious result of this effort would be a vine that would produce not one but many grapes. In fact, if the nurturing were done properly, there would be so many grapes produced that the grapes would have to be shared with others, as the harvest would be too much for just one person to consume.

The student then stated that to take any other course of action would be a "quick fix" and would never really satiate the desire for natural, "un-tampered with" grapes. If the difference between getting those grapes or settling for raisins (dry or re-hydrated) meant making additional investments, then that was the path to take. The outcome of the other solution would result in mildewed, soggy raisins. The student then commented, "The world offers too many opportunities for quick fixes and, in my book, mildew will never do. Even though I'm as impatient as the next person is, I'm not going to accept less. I know what I want."

The class fell silent. I asked, "What just happened?" One student commented that she now realized that she had taken the quick fix option in her current job situation. A man spoke up, with a smirk, and said that he was currently in a relationship that would qualify as accepting soggy raisins. One after another commented that there had been times when they had each opted for the soggy raisins. Interestingly, after every statement, the student displayed a defiant shift in their voice. Each steadfastly said, "Mildew will not do anymore."

The "old raisin" question really got the class thinking. How about you? *Does this provoke some new goals for you too?*

Provoking Success! (Coach's Review, Recommendations, Questions and Unreasonable Requests)

1. We have many opportunities for quick fix solutions.

2. Quick fix solutions rarely give us what we **truly** want or need.

3. Abundance comes about when we invest in what we truly want. Are you ready for abundance? Do you deserve abundance? What exactly is it that you do want?

4. The true test of a person's discipline in the realm of getting their needs met is whether there are more soggy raisins than grapes in his or her life.

5. **Action Item:** *Are you up for the test?* Make a list of all the soggy raisins you have in your life currently. Create an action plan to transition from having soggy raisins to having the grapes you want – include any time lines and support you'll need to make this possible.

Abundance means cultivation and cultivation means making disciplined choices. If you want abundance, know what you're truly choosing. – Coach John S. Nagy

8. Secretly Happy

Most people have no clue as to what they are truly seeking.
– Coach John S. Nagy

I bring up unusual pieces of information in my classes to get my students to think at a higher and deeper level than they have done before. Typically, those who really want to get something from the class have an "Aha!" moment. Here is an example of one of those "Aha!'s" – I start the class by asking, "Is there anyone here who wants to be truly happy?" It always elicits an instantaneous response from the group – "Yes! Indeed!" I then ask them if they would define what happiness means to them. The group then shares a potpourri of situations and things that bring them fulfillment, contentment and joy.

The interesting thing about what they share is what's missing from their descriptions. I can't say it's just one specific thing. What I can say for sure is that their descriptions do not really describe what happiness is at all. What I hear from them is not happiness; it's a *prerequisite* for happiness.

Hearing prerequisites for happiness rather than hearing what happiness is doesn't surprise me anymore. It's a rare occurrence for me to hear an accurate description of happiness. Most people give their response a lot of energy and not much thought.

For the most part, I believe our general population doesn't know what happiness really is. They usually have memories of feeling happy at one time or another. This is what they try to recall and describe when they are asked what happiness is. That's about as far they can go, and that's a sad commentary considering how many people pursue happiness so vigorously.

After hearing all these descriptions of prerequisites for happiness from my class, I throw in some eyebrow-raising bits of information.

The first tidbit I share is the root history of the word "happy." "Happy" comes from the same root word as "haphazard," "happenstance," and "happen." What these words all have in common is the root "hap." The word "hap" literally means "by chance." Contrary to the common dictionary meaning of the word "happiness," which is how most people use it in everyday life, happiness literally means "chance contentment."

What does this mean for people who want happiness? It means that they are looking for contentment to "happen" to them through no fault or design of their own. Contentment for these individuals occurs randomly. They are not causing it to occur. It is occurring sporadically, inconsistently, and with no predictability. The result is what you might guess; contentment occurs so "haphazardly" that you end up with an unhappy person most of the time.

By virtue of its haphazard nature, desiring "happiness" means desiring "random contentment." By its very definition, the moment you search for happiness you give up your right to create consciously contentment for and within yourself. When your choice is made, you no longer control when you will have contentment in your life for that is now presented randomly by situations you encounter. It's comparable to accepting soggy, mildewed raisins when what you really want is grapes.

After hearing this information from me, most of my students start clarifying what they want. Many of them don't like the idea of giving up personal control, particularly when it comes to their own contentment. Some even say they would forego happiness if it meant retaining control. Others suggest there has to be a way of having happiness without giving up control.

Before I tell them, "Yes, there is a way to have happiness without giving up control" and how it "Hap-pens," I add one more element to the mix. Most people never realize this next element. In fact, there are people who live their whole life, die, and go to the grave without getting a handle on this element. Still others do realize it and still struggle with it unsuccessfully. They never have its full potential blossoming within their world.

What is that missing element? Let's go back just a bit. Most people who complain that they are unhappy point their finger at what they think is the cause of their unhappiness. You hear these people saying things like, "If only I had this, that or the other (and the list is endless), then I'd be happy." They continually set up pre-conditions to their happiness by using "if – then" statements. What's more, they point to external sources and situations as being the cause of their discontent.

In other words, they choose to be unhappy with their current conditions and blame something or someone for causing those conditions to exist.

What they don't realize is that once a person has chosen to be unhappy, that's what they will be – *unhappy!* This is a direct reflection of that person's choices in their search for happiness. The very act of searching is a statement of discontent.

Is there a secret to having the happiness most people truly desire – true controllable contentment that occurs "for you" and not "to you?" The answer is "yes" and that secret is *choice.* If a person chooses to be contented with any situation, the outcome of that choice is to be happy – no matter what the situation. Once that choice of "being" occurs, she is going to "act" as happy people do and take actions that affirms her happiness. If she chooses to be happy and do happy things, what do you think the outcome will be? The result is obvious. She is going to have more people, things and situations that reinforce her happiness. If this 4-part sequence of events looks familiar – it is! This is an example of the components of an attitude talked about in a previous chapter.

You may say. "Coach, it can't be so simple as to just choose to be happy, can it?" My response is "Yes! It is that simple." When you understand the mechanism that causes results and outcomes, you can then make appropriate choices to cause the results and outcomes you want.

It's so simple that it's hard for some people to see. *It's a matter of choice.* Choose to be content with the people, situations and things in your life, whether they occur by design or default. Once you make your choice to be content, you're going to behave, act and perceive life in a contented manner – no matter what you cause or don't cause in life. What used to cause upset will lose its power within this new frame of reference. Invariably, you will surround yourself with people, situations and things that re-enforce you as the source of your contentment. Exercising this and you become a person who sees opportunity for contentedness in all situations.

If you think that this sounds too easy and too simple, you may not be looking for the opportunity it affords you. It is true that this will take continuous practice and firm commitment to reframe your experiences. The effort you make will bring some unbelievable rewards and astonishing results.

Coach's Note: *Don't be fooled into thinking that contentment focused happiness means not aspiring to change things that can be changed. It doesn't. It merely means you're not going to be discontent with the vast majority of what you have and don't have before you. In addition, if your present path for seeking happiness is not working for you, what would you need to provoke you toward a more contenting path?*

Provoking Success! (Coach's Review, Recommendations, Questions and Unreasonable Requests)

1. Understand and believe that happiness starts with choice. True choice is internal.

2. Choose to be content with life so your happiness won't depend on what you cause in life and what you *don't* cause in life.

3. Strive to be a person who sees *all* occurrences as opportunities to find contentment.

4. Play your role authentically. Respond and react to all situations with contentment and a sincere interest in looking for further opportunity for the same.

5. Reap the results!

6. **Action Item:** Start a journal and keep score. Define a "win" as any opportunity seen that would lead to further contentment.

7. Find value in what is before you – no matter how small.

Coach's Note: *This discipline takes practice, so its impact is gradual as you continue to find more opportunity to practice it. If you think this whole thing sounds phony, try this next time you don't like something: Ask yourself what you don't like about it. Then ask yourself what you can like about it or – even better – what opportunity this person, this thing, or situation can offer you. Contentment comes in different forms and most of us have trained ourselves not to see very many of them, so sometimes opportunities to find contentment have to "whack us upside the head with a 2 by 4 beam of wood." I'm hoping this chapter will save you a few "whacks" and keep you free from feeling "board."*

Not happy yet? Make better choices! – Coach John S. Nagy

Uncommon Personal Refinement

Begin with the end-in-mind and remember:
you are the end-in-mind.
                                        – Coach John S. Nagy

9. Playing It Straight

Are you quite a character? – Coach John S. Nagy

Over the years, I've told many stories to clients and friends. I find stories to be very useful devices to convey concepts needing to be shared. One of these stories has had a profound effect on those with whom I've shared it. The story is based on a conversation that occurred back in my engineering days while I was working at a local electronics plant.

At that time, I was continuously looking at "classified ads" to see what other engineering jobs were out there. Sometimes, for fun, I'd tell the engineers I worked with the kinds of people other businesses were looking for. Doing this usually stirred the conversational pot and filled the time during lunch. One day while I was checking out the classifieds, I saw a position for an engineer at an entertainment-oriented business near Orlando, Florida. I chuckled at the thought of working at such a place and shouted over to my friend that I was going to send them a resume. He smirked and said, "Fat chance they'd hire you!"

Taken back a bit at his comment, I asked him if he thought I didn't have the expertise to do the job. He said it had nothing to do with my talents; it was *my mustache that would keep the door closed to me*.

"What's my mustache got to do with working at that place?" I asked.

He told me that the entertainment industry in Florida has an exemption from the Equal Opportunity Employment Act and can choose to hire or not hire people based on their appearance. Florida employment law allows for specific hiring for specific roles. This was in spite of the fact that this was a right-to-work state.

I bellowed "Aha! That has nothing to do with me being hired as an engineer. That has to do with actors."

He didn't flinch. He asked me if I remembered seeing the "Casting Director" signs outside some of these theme parks. I said "yes" and added, "I thought it was just a cute touch to add to the ambiance of the park."

He said that it was not just a "nice touch." It was a way for them to have control over whom they hired and didn't hire. If I looked around, nowhere would I find a sign saying "personnel director" because there wasn't one, only "casting directors."

"So what's with the casting director thing?" I asked.

"Simple put," he said, "they wouldn't hire you as an engineer. They're not interested in hiring 'personnel'. They're interested in hiring someone to fill a role. Hence, they would hire you as an actor who played the part of an engineer. They'd give you a script for being an engineer and expect you to learn and follow it to the letter. You'd play the role so they would have the 'character' they needed to fill that part in their show.

Moreover, part of that role would be what you were supposed to look like and what kind of attitude your character would have while following the script. They want your looks, your attitude, and your behavior to fit perfectly with their script. In addition, since you'd be paid a salary, they'd expect you to play the part at both work and when you were away from work. That way they could demand that you didn't play a different part whenever you were away from their show."

"That's crazy," I said. "If they hired me to play the part of a cartoon character, how could I play that part while I was out to dinner with my family and friends?"

"John! Get it. They don't want you to play the role of that cartoon character when you have the costume off. They want you to play the role of a cartoon character *actor*. This way it doesn't matter if you've taken the costume off. They really want you to "be" in the role twenty-four hours a day.

"Why would they want to have such control?" I asked.

"How would you like your cast members doing things that are controversial and winding up with their faces plastered all over the press with your show's name associated with them? Not too smooth, eh? They don't like this possibility either, so, as a salaried cast member who is playing a part, you assure them that you're a good actor and that this wouldn't happen."

I snarled, "That sounds so false!"

He smiled. "Not if you're playing the part authentically. You see, they are not trying to hire people who can just 'play' the part. They're looking for people who can 'be' the part. They want the person to be so authentically into the role that everyone who encounters them will think that they *are* the part they're playing. In fact, if they hired you as an engineer, they'd expect you to be the part so authentically that *you actually believed* you are an engineer. Only the casting director and you would know that you're merely a great actor playing the role they hired you to fill. The tag line on all this is that they wouldn't hesitate to find someone else to fill the role if you were unable or unwilling to follow the script exactly to achieve the characterization they wanted. It's a simple game they play – with simple rules. And that's why they wouldn't hire you, John."

"Are you saying that I couldn't pull it off?" I said.

He said, "Maybe you could. But not with that mustache."

"What does that have to do with it?"

"Sorry John," he smiled, "all the roles they have to offer don't call for an engineer with a mustache."

Ouch! Talk about attention to detail!

— — —

I share this story with clients who are struggling to play a specific role in their business or in their personal life. What triggers me to tell it is when I notice that what they say they want and what I see them doing doesn't match up.

Most people don't realize that to have a professional or personal characterization in their lives deliberately, they must follow a specific path. That path is no less than a script or road map that must be followed without wavering. Any waver in the script will change the character or outcome desired. The greatest force that contributes to wavering is how the person flip-flops in what they choose to "be" from one moment to the next. The "being" is the role they have chosen to play.

The three components one must be aware of in order to obtain the outcome they desire are:

1. the role
2. the script
3. the characterization

The first component is what you choose to "**be**." It's the "identity, mask or persona" you wish to portray. *The first "rule of roles" is that what you choose to "be" is the role you take on. The second "rule of roles" is that if you plan to be one thing and really are being another, the other is the true role you're playing.* Many "take on" a role and think they are truly playing it. Upon careful examination of the outcome, realize the role they were actually playing was different from what they thought. If what I'm saying isn't clear, hang in there. I'll share an example of what I mean soon.

The second component is the script and is what you "**do**." It is known by a variety of names including: road map, instruction set, program, guidelines, "rules of the road," response-abilities and the "path." *The first "rule of scripts" is that actions are dictated by the energy of "being."* In other words, every action that a person takes is governed by the role they are playing.

Most people might think this would be confining and produce a way of life lacking spontaneity. The truth is that the script doesn't confine; the *role* is the restricting agent. That's why the better you know who you are choosing to *be*; the easier it becomes to play your part authentically. If you know who you truly "are" then any behavior you exhibit will be genuine to that "being." Any other possible behavior won't even be considered since it is not what you would "do." This also means that all possible behavior that is genuine to "who you are" is now readily available to you and can be displayed in infinite ways.

Troubling behaviors only occur when a player flip-flops about the role they wish to play after they've supposedly committed themselves to the path.

Let's take a look at an example. A person chooses to get into a business providing legal services. After choosing to play the role of "a business owner," that person then settles into *not* playing that specific role but another role called "attorney." They may think they're following the right script – the business owner, but they're actually following a different script – that of the attorney. The script of the business owner requires different actions than that of an attorney. So, while this person is following the path of being the attorney, all the actions that aren't getting done by him, as the business owner, start creating problems. Problematic business outcomes are guaranteed if the role of business owner is played by a person who has abdicated his or her responsibilities as the business owner. (As you might have speculated, this same pattern occurs outside of work too!)

The "mark we make" comes from the actions we take. Characterization, the third component, dictates the results, outcomes, consequences and impacts that come about by our following a specific script. It's what you eventually "**have**." Many people don't realize that the results they see before them came about because of what they chose to "be." Hence, *the first "rule of character": results flow from your actions (and inactions!).* The best way to evaluate a role that you've been playing is to look at the character you have. If the character is not what you desire, the role that you're playing needs to be changed.

The interesting thing that emerges from all this is that once you understand what the role-script-character concept is all about, you see that it has more to do with life and living it than it has to do with some amusement park near Orlando.

Coach's Note: *The role you choose to take on and "be" provokes the life you will act out and have!*

Provoking Success! (Coach's Review, Recommendations, Questions and Unreasonable Requests)

1. What you choose to "be" is the role you take on.

2. Actions are dictated by the energy of "being." Whatever role you're choosing to play in life requires a specific script to be followed. Waver in the role and you waver in the script.

3. Results are obtained from your actions. The more authentic the role is for you, the better chance you have of getting the characterization you desire. Waver from the script and you change the character.

4. Playing any part falsely, no matter how slight the in authenticity, will always bring about characterizations contrary to those called for by the script.

5. People (family, friends, businesses, etc.) who are looking for a specific character will replace anyone who cannot follow the script well enough to bring that character about.

6. Character is the mark we make – the results of who we are. What we *have* is a result of the character *we put forth*.

7. **Action Item:** Create a list of your roles, actions and results. If the results are not what you want, evaluate your role in the situations that brought about the results. What role can you play to bring about different results? Write out on paper "what must you be" and what script (actions) you must play out.

Coach's Note: *I no longer have a mustache (and it no longer "has" me).*

> *Any 'having' starts with a specific 'being.'*
> *– Coach John S. Nagy*

10. Getting Off Your But!

I'd love to tell you more, but... – Coach John S. Nagy

A meeting occurred a few years back that brought my attention to something profound: A client and I were brainstorming a group of interrelated challenges that were happening in her life.

After about fifteen minutes into our discussion, I became aware of a pattern: She would share something that, for me, pointed to an obvious solution. I would make a suggestion to help her realize a way to brainstorm a solution creatively. No sooner had I made the suggestion to get the brainstorming going than I'd hear something from her that rang a familiar, unnerving bell.

I had heard this tolling bell before. Almost a decade earlier, as an undergraduate student in college, I sat in a supposedly instructive class on brainstorming. The professor explained to the class what brainstorming was about and how we could benefit our co-workers and ourselves by using it to solve problems.

He strongly emphasized the importance of respect for each other—that we never shoot down *any* idea offered, no matter how our preconceived notions might judge those ideas because doing so would only discourage further creativity and sharing. He suggested the best way to brainstorm was to keep ourselves open to the ideas of others. We thought the theory sounded great and were eager to try it out in class.

The professor offered to demonstrate the concept by presenting us with a problem he was having funding a project. Sad to say, I got a chance to see someone, the professor, who, even as well versed in the theory of brainstorming as he was, "botch it" to the max. Immediately after explaining the problem, students rushed to share a storm of ideas. Some were truly good, some perhaps not so good. What surprised me were the Professor's negative responses to the questionable ideas. I realized then how good brainstorming sessions could go astray and how, even a person well versed in theory, can be pulled along with that wayward current.

This memory came up during the coaching session with my client because I saw her going down that same path. It was profound. I actually witnessed the mechanism, the string that pulled her away from true brainstorming and that string was a thick one. I started to keep count of how frequently that "string" appeared in our conversation (and I included in my count some interesting variations on her basic theme). After about ten minutes of keeping count on a napkin, I began to laugh. My client stopped talking and smiled nervously, puzzled, even as I made another strike. She asked me what was so amusing. I said that I'd had a "eureka" moment about ten minutes before and thought a recorded count would drive home the point. Her interest was piqued and she wanted to know what I had been counting, making it a great teaching moment. I shared with her the pattern I saw in our chat: Together, we would pinpoint a problem. Then, we threw out a suggestion to overcome it. Next, while she would quickly affirm these suggestions, she would just as quickly shoot them down. This occurred repeatedly— the sheer pervasiveness of the pattern was stalling all our progress in brainstorming. Hence, she continued to be stuck.

She asked me how I had noticed this. I said it was her continual "yeah, but..." that made it so obvious. No matter how well we stirred the pot to get potential solutions and get actions cooking, she always did something, a "yeah, but, or something like it, to blow out the flame, so the stew never got hot enough to boil. Her behavior was no longer frustrating; it had crossed over to being humorously annoying!

My keeping count showed how ingrained within her this behavior was. She asked how many times she'd said, "yeah, but..." during those ten minutes. Her mouth dropped open in astonishment when I told her "Twenty times."

During the next hour, we discussed the phrase, "Yeah, but..." in depth. We discussed the full ramifications of "Yeah, but…" and sibling phrases she was using to cover the obvious discounting (put-downs) of her ideas that she was doing to herself. She asked if it would be okay to use the word "however" instead of "but." I said "Sure, if you want the same effect. It's only a bigger 'but.'" She smiled.

The words we choose don't matter more than the intent they convey. If a word or a phrase discounts or does a "put down" on something that was just said, it should be avoided. This went double in her case, since she used some variation of "Yeah, but..." in just about every sentence that came out of her mouth.

In frustration, she asked me what she could do to change the pattern of discounting that was so ingrained in her behavior. I said the first thing to do was to become aware of the words she chose. Words and phrases like "but," and, "yet," "although," "the thing is," "if only," and "however" are all discounting words that place limits on and stifle what is being discussed or thought about. They indicate "exclusiveness" (being excluded) rather than "inclusiveness" (being included) in communications.

This is not to say that these words and phrases are not useful and appropriate at times. They are and "yes" I do use them myself. The point to remember about them is that *excessive* use creates limiting ways of perceiving one's self and one's associated stuck points. Those attempting to be of help are often forced into a "tooth-pulling" exercise with the person whose self-limiting thinking patterns are stuck in high gear.

Can you imagine going through life with limiting and discounting words & phrases continuously going on in your thinking or worse yet, coming out of your mouth every 30 seconds?

During that coaching session, the second recommendation I made to her was to replace the limiting and discounting phrases with the word "and." Using "and" provokes one to use creativity, inclusiveness and ownership in one's thinking and behavior. She smiled and said that was what she really needed to get out of the slump. That's when *I* smiled.

Provoking Success! (Coach's Review, Recommendations, Questions and Unreasonable Requests)

1. Become aware of your own self-limiting and self-discounting words and phrases. Write them out.

2. Commit to detoxifying your thinking and conversation as a way of changing your beliefs and attitudes into healthier shape.

3. **Action Item:** Stop using all these negative phrases for a minimum of thirty days. When and if you slip up, do NOT berate yourself. Doing that will reinforce the negatives you are working to replace. Instead, ask yourself, "What can I learn from this experience to help me do even better?" What's the lesson?

4. **Action Item:** Provoke yourself toward using the word "and" anytime the word "but" (or any of its siblings) come to your lips. Do this until you master your "but" thinking.

Coach's Note: *When these negative phrases do come up, excuse yourself, then go back and rephrase it so it becomes inclusive, shows appreciation and indicates your full ownership of the situation and statement.*

B.U.T. (Behold the Underlying Truth) – Coach John S. Nagy

11. I'll have a Double!

Mixed messages often convey double standards.
— Coach John S. Nagy

A few years back I had occasion to visit with a fellow business traveler and share a delightful breakfast at a local nook. Most folks who came here ordered Bagels and tea and I was no exception.

My partner that morning was an ex-professor who had taught at the business school of a university for years and had finally established his own business. "And that business would be?" I asked.

"Stock Broker," he said with a tone that complemented his playful grin.

I smiled back, mimicking the same playful manner. With the immediate "first words" tension released, we preceded to sit and enjoy a very pleasant breakfast, moving easily back and forth in the conversation and sharing the events that had led each of us up to this moment.

The two of us sat there – he, new in business as a stockbroker trying to make connections to build his business and enjoying his mid-50's without burning himself out; me, with the exception of having a few more years in business and a coaching focus, looking for the very same things: connections and building my business without burning-out. We embraced our exchange with vigor and could not have been in better company.

We talked intently for an hour, covering our backgrounds, highlighting here and there how we helped our clients and sharing our attempts to make a mark in the world. At the end of our time together, we transitioned elegantly to the traditional

"Let's get together in a month and see how we can put together a win/win scenario." I think we both enjoyed the meeting and I believe each of us envisioned benefits from the possible business connection.

With the beginnings of a connection made and concluded, we sequenced into "departing" mode. Parting can sometimes be an awkward moment, but neither of us had a hint of angst about it. Both of us qualified as "master departers," having shaken many a hand before.

It was at that moment in our concluding motions that I decided to do something I had trained for all my business years. He knew what was coming and danced skillfully with me as I put out a traditional request for names. "Asking for leads" is a common strategy used by those of us involved in businesses that are dependent on networking as the major means of marketing.

He focused intently on my eyes, paused strategically for just a fraction of a second and then smiled with the same playfulness he had at the beginning of our conversation. This time though I saw a cautionary message emerging in his eyes. "John," he said with an apologetic tone, "I'd love to give you some leads and will do so as soon as I get to know you better. In fact, I make it a policy to do this once I've spent enough time with someone. I've learned over the years that I can't refer someone without knowing him or her better. It's standard practice for me. I hope you understand."

I said I fully understood his position and respected his standard for doing business in this manner. I quickly continued in another direction by thanking him for meeting with me. The execution was flawless, or so I thought.

As we shook hands, again sharing appreciation, he said, "You know. I'm impressed that you practice what you preach. Asking for leads is just good business practice. I guess I should take your lead and start making it part of all my exchanges." I grinned and commented in the affirmative.

He added, "By the way, if you know of anyone in the area who needs a broker, could you send them my way?"

Without skipping a beat, I smiled warmly and said, "Why certainly. I'd love to give you all the leads I can. In fact, I make it a policy to do this whenever the opportunity presents itself."

I paused and that pause rang as loud as a three-alarm fire. I could see that he heard it too, by the response in his eyes.

I stared back at him; his hand still gripped in mine, and provocatively added, "Just one question. Shall I use my standard, or yours?"

Provoking Success! (Coach's Review, Recommendations, Questions and Unreasonable Requests)

1. **Action Item:** Standards are those limits to which we hold ourselves accountable. Write about them until you're clear about the standards by which you're living and working.

2. **Action Item:** Boundaries are those limits to which we hold others accountable. Write about them until you're clear about the boundaries you're communicating to others, in both personal and professional settings.

3. **Action Item:** Make sure that your standards and boundaries are equitable. Don't expect more from others than you would expect from yourself.

4. **Action Item:** When are your expectations of others more then what you would expect from yourself? Explore the "why" in this!

Know your limits! – Coach John S. Nagy

12. Bogus Screen Savers

Labels can mislead and often convey a false sense of assurance.
– Coach John S. Nagy

Often, the irony of our choices shows up in the most commonly accepted everyday things. The other day I was in a long-time coaching client's office, when I noticed something odd out of the corner of my eye: On his desktop computer monitor a randomly moving pattern was swirling across the screen

I recognized it immediately as one of those screen saver patterns that some people program into their computers to come up automatically after a designated time. The original intent of these programs was to limit the time the monitor continued to show an active screen with those little glowing dots after you stopped using your computer. If you didn't have a screen saver program running and left the monitor sitting with the same screen showing, eventually the pattern would etch itself into the faceplate of your computer screen. After a while, the screen would not be able to show a clean representation due to the burned phosphorous. It would not render the screen useless, just noticeably scarred.

Of course, what we have today is nowhere near this simple design or intent. Many of today's screen savers do everything *but* save your screen. They create all sorts of interesting, eye-catching patterns that keep your attention *and continue* to illuminate the screen's phosphor.

One day, while working with a client, I asked him why he took the time to put a screen saver on his machine. He said the reason was obvious, to save the screen on his monitor. He added, "Isn't that what they're supposed to do?"

I said, "Yes, that's what they're supposed to do. The problem is some do and some don't." The one he had chosen kept the whole screen active and only changed a small section of screen from one moment to the next. The result was that the ratio of time the screen was engaged in a highly illuminated static pattern compared to the time when the monitor was engaged in a slight squiggly swirl made little difference in preventing long-term damage to the screen.

My client said, "Huh?"

I said, "To save your screen, you must choose a screen saver that actually does its job. To prevent screen burns, it must either shut your screen off or have a bare minimum displayed. Even at a bare minimum, there needs to be a pattern that travels around against a black background, so no one area of the screen is continually active.

He said, "Oh! That make's sense." and proceeded to go into his screen saver options and choose a pattern that did just that. He smiled, thanked me and we got back to the original coaching conversation.

This brings me back to my point for sharing this story: Sometimes we choose to take an action, with the best of intentions, and fail to achieve the objective because we didn't check our work to see if it did what it promised to do.

My client's screen saver was a typical example. Many people take action to put something in place to help them avoid possible future problems. Their choice actually brings the problem about because they didn't evaluate it and think it through beforehand. There are many possible choices available. Many options have labels promote themselves as being "screen savers." Most people make selections based on the "label name" thinking that the product or service offered is closely attached to the name. Some people never receive the action that the name implied. This is evident in many of the things promoted in our culture.

Here's a typical example of this: "Fat Free" implies that the product before us is *health and diet-oriented.* A quick read of the product's ingredients will often reveal that the product doesn't support this at all. All it could possibly do is *ruin our appetite because of* knowing *what's in it. If this were the case, why would we want to buy it?*

Usually, people who have chosen poorly failed to do a reality-check before they made the choice and then discovered they had to live with the unfortunate outcomes. Before you choose to trust that the label on a product (or service) will bring the desired results, check it out. Often times we're so distracted by the bells and whistles described on the label that we don't realize we're being burned just like our computer screen. It's difficult to live with the burns and scars caused by these choices. This is why it's so valuable to "re-evaluate" our choices from time to time. Provoke yourself toward thinking past the labels you are being shown and become action and result sensitive. You'll be glad you did.

Coach's Note: *Today's screens are much better at preventing burn patterns then those of yesteryear – but saving screens was never really the reason for this discussion, was it?*

Provoking Success! (Coach's Review, Recommendations, Questions and Unreasonable Requests)

1. **Action Item:** Take the time to look at your surroundings.
2. **Action Item:** Ask yourself if what you have is what you intended to have.
3. **Action Item:** Take an additional step and ask yourself, "Is what I have going on in my life truly supporting what I want to bring about?"
4. **Action Item:** Create a list of all your bogus "screen savers" – things, situations and people who claim to benefit you in certain ways – when in fact they're not.
5. **Action Item:** Start making adjustments to bring the genuine articles into your life.
6. **Action Item:** Continue to review your life periodically to see if other bogus screen savers have crept in when you were busy focusing your attention elsewhere.
7. **Action Item:** Ask others that you trust to be truthful if there are things that you communicate through word or action that are just as bogus as the screensavers you're trying to eliminate or correct. Listen to them with sincerity. Take appropriate action on what you hear.

Just because they call it "fat free" doesn't mean it's good for you. – Coach John S. Nagy

13. Busyness Investments

High upfront investments in relationships could mean long-term high maintenance. – Coach John S. Nagy

I've coached many business owners over the years. One business owner was particularly fun to coach because most of the people who used his services really had no idea what his business was really about! It's not that they were conscious of their ignorance. They just never really thought about what was being presented to them. (I'll let you imagine for yourself what his business might be.)

As a business coach, I like the opportunity to open some eyes when a case like this happens. The light that goes on behind their eyes when they "get it" is an absolute thrill. Unfortunately, some folks extinguish this light almost immediately after it turns on. They don't want to think too much about the light, because thinking about it would mean they'd have to drastically change the way they operate their business.

So the information I share with them, showing what their business is *really* all about, has to do with the basics of their operation and the choices that move them forward into continued success; it is the premise upon which they build their business.

The basics I teach to one particular client about producing a viable income stream are no different from what I would teach for any business that relies on personnel and sales for growth. In such businesses, there are three levels of activity that can create income.

To be successful in this type of business, the **first level** of activity requires business operators to *move inventory*. This means that they must make sure they are selling a product (and/or providing a service) to people who are willing to purchase it. Although most people call these people "customers, purchasers or buyers," I call these people "investors." No matter what we call them, these people invest in the product/service for their personal or "end" use. In other words, from a business standpoint, the first level requires you to have a product/service to sell and that you in fact sell it to others.

Success doesn't stop here, because the **second level** of activity requires business operators to expand their operations by finding others who are willing to purchase inventory and move it along by selling it – to other investors. These additional people, brought in for second level purposes, are themselves investors in that they are invested in finding others who will 1) invest in (purchase) inventory and 2) invest in the process of finding still others who will invest in the product/service for end use. In other words, from a business standpoint, the second level requires you to find others who are willing to do what you were doing at the first level and that you continue to do first level work yourself.

The **third level** of business activity requires the business operator to find others who are willing to invest in finding others who are willing to invest in second level activities. These are: 1) purchase inventory to sell, 2) finding others who will invest in inventory and 3) invest in the process of finding others who are willing to invest in the product/service for end use. In other words, from a business standpoint, the third level focuses on finding "finders" while still maintaining involvement in finding "sellers" and "buyers."

Does this sound a bit confusing? You bet it does. That's why many people never succeed in the business. They don't see the basic commonality of all three levels. Let's make it simpler:

No matter what level you're involved in, there is always a common aspect: the "investor." (Using the term "customer" may take focus off the need to have investors.) What makes business operations work are investors, and they must be present at every level of business activities. The first level must be stocked with investors who are called "buyers." The second level needs investors who are called "sellers." The third and last level needs investors who are called "recruiters" or "finders." No matter what you call them, remember that they're all investors.

This is why it's so much fun to coach people in these businesses. If they "get" the simple fact that investors make their businesses grow, then from that moment on, as serious business professionals, they will focus all their activities on dealing with investors. It's just good business sense.

The same goes for any other business. Good businesses will go for the investor every time. This means only dealing with people who are willing to invest something they consider valuable into the mix. Anything less would mark that person as being a non-investor and not worth working with.

How does one determine whether a person is an investor or not? It's simple. Look for commitment. If someone won't commit to investing some aspect of their valuable resources in your direction like time, energy, money, or spirit, it's a good indication they're not an investor. To be a success in this type of business, you must have investors.

Coach's Note: *Proceed with caution. Do not confuse a verbal statement of "willingness to invest" with an actual investment. Talk is cheap! You'll know a true investment by **action or follow through**. If nothing is occurring—inaction – you probably are dealing with an un-invested person.*

However, suppose you put in the effort to "convince" a person to invest. You might think this effort is a good investment on your part and that you're in store for a good return. Be forewarned that the amount of energy you *expend up front* to "convince" another person to invest in you and your product/service is a good indication of how much energy you'll have to expend to *maintain* that person on the back-end – as a continuing investor!

Now, you might say this has nothing to do with your business and you could be right. Please evaluate it before you dismiss this principle as not applicable to your situation. Ask yourself the following question: "What value am I offering to others that would create a desire to invest in my direction? Alternatively, how about: Who or what do I invest in that doesn't give me a return on my investment? Yet, one more: On average, am I dealing with a majority of investors or non-investors?

When you understand that all business – and life for that matter – is merely an offer and acceptance, that is, an exchange of products and services with others who are willing to invest in you, and you in them, then you start to do business – and life – in a completely different way. You start to invest yourself at a whole other level. You *don't* invest in people who are unwilling to invest themselves. Those interactions or transactions that give poor returns are no longer invested in. To do so just wouldn't provoke good business.

Provoking Success! (Coach's Review, Recommendations, Questions and Unreasonable Requests)

1. View yourself as an investor. View your business and your life as a series of investments. View all your customers, personnel and peers as investors.

2. **Action Item:** Create a list to better understand when a person is investing & when they are not.

3. **Action Item:** Use your list. Invest in investors. Divest from the un-invested and only invest for higher returns.

If you invest, make sure you're clear on what you're expecting in return. – Coach John S. Nagy

14. Fulfilling Fulfillment

Coach Nagy's First Rule of Sponges:
They never give back what they take.

Are there times when you feel unfulfilled and want more return for your personal and professional investments? Rest assured you can have what you want. There's a cost though. You have to learn to put up with less!

That's what I tell my clients when I hear them complaining about not having enough time, energy, or other resources. I know from experience that more than 90 percent of the cause of this complaint is not due to lack of resources. It's due to a *waste* of resources that causes them to appear scarce. When this seeming scarcity occurs, stress levels typically become overwhelming. That's where I come in. I put them on a program to evaluate how efficiently they are using their resources. This starts the process of taking more effective actions, which means relief and fulfillment are nearby. (**Hint:** *This concept links nicely with the chapter on effectiveness and efficiency!*)

One technique I offer to clients to get this process kick-started, both professionally and personally, is to create a list of *sponges. Sponges* are those situations, people, and things that contribute little or nothing to our well-being. Included in this are investments of our time, money, energy, and spirit that show poor returns. In essence, sponges suck our resources from us and leave us feeling empty.

Intermittently occurring sponges can be dealt with minor impact in our lives; however, when we deal with them constantly, we create a problem that gets in our way. Life becomes stressful. What adds to the problem is that our threshold for experiencing sponge-type activity increases every time we make an exception to our usual standards.

Coach's Note: *"Standards" are those limits to which we hold ourselves accountable.*

When we lower our personal and professional standards, we actually train ourselves to tolerate increasing amounts of being "sponged on." The result: *sponges become larger, there are more of them and they will drain more from you.*

For various reasons, we sometimes make exceptions to our standards with people we encounter, work with, or sometimes, even those we live with. We therefore learn to: 1) put up with; 2) take on; and 3) begrudgingly accept things, behavior and situations that are truly not ours to handle. Instead of allowing others to deal with and learn how to solve their own unmet needs, boundary issues, unfinished projects, frustrations, and other self-caused problems, we step in and dedicate our resources to "helping them." In other words, we choose to allow ourselves to be dragged down by sponges. In addition, we can sometimes "cripple" these same people from the satisfaction of learning that they really can solve their own problems.

Sometimes *we're* the sponges and we allow things to go unfinished, contribute to accumulations (packed closets/garages, clutter, un-filed paperwork, things bought and never used, etc.) that get in the way or we ignore, like maintenance or repair needs. All these situations contribute to resource drainage.

This is why I request my clients list their sponges. Once the list is created, their next action item is to identify those sponges that can be knocked off the list immediately. Shortening the list can be accomplished in a variety of ways.

One method is simply to stop providing actions that support sponges. One of my clients complained about having high maintenance clients. The time that he spent supporting their needless queries prevented him from prospecting elsewhere. By identifying the drain on his time and the cause for the drain, he was able to remove the drain quickly. By notifying those clients of his new support policy (what he would and wouldn't do any longer), he was able to increase the amount of time for prospecting and reduce the energy and time drains caused by his needless support activity.

Another method is to identify those things that are not completed and decide immediately whether to "cut them loose" and move on, or (even better) to complete them and put them to rest once and for all. This may be a project that was never finished or a simple thing like cleaning out a closet. The main thing is to become aware of how much time, money, energy, and spirit you put into maintaining these items in their incomplete state with no return.

If you want to feel the difference that "putting a sponge to rest" can make, identify and then put a simple sponge to rest and evaluate your body response when you finish. Most people feel emotions ranging from mild contentment to downright delight, sprinkled liberally with "relief." If you know anything about motivation, you know that these are building blocks needed to get the ball rolling.

Next time you start chomping at the "anxiety bit" due to resource drains and start mumbling the mantra ("Too much to do, too little time, money and energy to do it,"), think about the following irony: being filled with unfulfilling activities is different than being fulfilled. Get your resource usage back on track. Provoke a change for the better – get your list going.

Provoking Success! (Coach's Review, Recommendations, Questions and Unreasonable Requests)

1. Admit that you have sponges in your life.

2. **Action Item:** Identify the areas in your life that are unfulfilling.

3. **Action Item:** Create a list of items that contribute little to no return to your well-being.

4. Decide what you want to continue supporting and what you want to stop supporting.

5. **Action Item:** Create an action plan to improve the return on those items you want to continue supporting.

6. **Action Item:** Create an action plan to remove those items you no longer want to support.

When you minimize the sponges in your life, you have more of everything you truly need. – Coach John S. Nagy

15. Oddly Possible

Dream awesomely! Savor grand visions! Safeguard your success! Invest mightily in supportive measures! Improve your odds of winning. – Coach John S. Nagy

There is a real possibility you may put this book down right after reading this chapter and never pick it up again. I warn you ahead of time since this is possible. Is it probable? Only you can answer that question. The truth behind personal and professional change (the kinds of change this book is all about) is that most *fancied* change is not going to occur or if it does occur, it will not be long lasting. Change, although constant, shackles itself to habit – behavior constantly manifested by our inner autopilot to help us keep consistency in our lives.

You might now be hearing that inner voice screaming inside you saying something like "Coach! Are you **insane?** Why in the world would you be shooting yourself in the foot? Wouldn't sharing this kind of information be more likely to discourage me rather than encourage me?" My response is simple: Yeah, you're right – if such mind chatter easily discourages you.

As you might have gathered from reviewing past efforts to create change, yours or others, change, the kind that lasts, is not for wimps. The fact is people who want to change for the better arm themselves with a compelling vision of possibility. As an added "success protection," they also want to arm themselves with the knowledge of probability. These folks love to be able to imagine what is possible for them – and for others. They also want to rest assured that they have **safeguarded** themselves **against failure!**

How do they do this? Better yet, how can **you** do this? Good questions to ask.

I can tell you how and I can show you how. Will it have an impact on your success? Only you can answer that question.

Before you do that, let's examine a few of the elements in a simple game of chance. Many people have shaken a pair of dice in their hands and used them to determine what they can and cannot do when playing certain games. With a pair of dice, you can roll 36 possible number combinations. The outcome of what you roll dictates the next actions you can take. On the surface, it's simple enough.

As we look more deeply into this game, we find either through trial and error *or* through evaluation that for each roll of the dice there are specific odds that favor what the outcome of each roll will be. We start to see that if we want to obtain a specific combination of numbers, we have specific probabilities or odds with which to contend. For instance, the highest probability of the numbers on the dice adding up to seven is 16.7 percent. Every other combination of numbers has a lesser probability of happening. If you restate this as the probability of each roll *not* being a seven, you quickly see that the odds are 83.3 percent against you getting a seven on any roll of the dice. That means that there's a 5 to 1 ratio against you winning.

Yes. It's a numbers game and it illustrates to you that any game you engage in will have odds with which you must contend.

Now, if we connect this concept back into the original discussion revolving around creating change, you might start to see that change is possible. Moreover, you might also see that the probability - the odds - of it occurring consistently is directly dependant on how you design your support system to have the best odds of bringing it about.

A professional who wants to increase the number of clients or customers she serves will work to illustrate an example of this. If she focuses her attention on being able to deliver better services or products, word has a better chance to get around that she is the one to contact for obtaining such things. Does this mean that she is going to improve her odds of success? Maybe yes. Would improving her marketing systems so that more people know that her product and services are available increase her odds even more? All things being equal, the answer would be "yes." Would her reading a romance novel to escape the pressures of looming failure improve the odds? Most likely not, unless it's done "off hours" and it somehow "recharges" her to better perform while she's on the job.

If her overall habits do not support improving the odds, the odds are going to go against her. If her habits consistently sabotage her efforts to improve, the odds of her success are greatly diminished.

In another situation, a man envisions his wife to be something she is currently not. He shares this vision with her and she begrudgingly commits herself to bringing about the change for his sake even though it is not her own vision for herself. No further actions other than occasional "lip service" are given to this arrangement. He nags her occasionally; she makes a meager effort at first but slacks off once his naggings lessens. This continues ad nausea for some time. Fifty years later, he's still holding on to his vision for her and she is still who she is. The only thing that has changed is the bitterness within them both due to fifty years of embattlement.

Why didn't it work? The system they designed was not meant to bring about change. It was to deepen rejection of who they were to each other. If they had focused on changing themselves toward what each of them wanted for themselves, the probability of successful transformation would have increased tremendously. The reason for this is that no one truly has control of another human being. You only have influence and that is *if and only if*

the other party desires to accept the influence you have to offer.
If they don't accept it, then you have no influence over them.

Now you might tell me that you have certain leveraging devices
such as finances, friendships with others, and other assorted
common grounds that can influence them to do what you want
them to do. Sure, you may have control over some
environmental factors. Truthfully, it's still really up to them to
decide if they are willing to accept or reject those influences for
whatever reasons they have for themselves. Participation in your
game is still up to them.

In both situations, you are participating in a game with certain
odds. It is possible to influence the outcome of sales or
relationships. Is it probable? You have to look at the odds!

Keep in mind the following: This information is not shared to
depress or discourage you or to sabotage your dreams. It is gifted
to you to provide insight into what creates success. If it provokes
you, so much the better – especially if you accept this influence
as beneficial since it increases the odds of success in your favor!

How can you further improve your odds of success? Take this
information and **apply it** toward what you have envisioned for
yourself. Delve into what your habits will do to either support or
sabotage your success. Look at the numbers! Project what you
see as an outcome and design your success support system to
encourage you toward your goals. Both quality and quantity
should be measured to reflect your progress back to you. Most of
all learn to know the difference between possibility and
probability.

All continuous success is the execution of habits that provoke
higher odds that favor specific desired outcomes. If you find that
your successes are inconsistent, your habits provoked that, too!

Provoking Success! (Coach's Review, Recommendations, Questions and Unreasonable Requests)

1. For any envisioned possibility, there is an associated probability.
2. Just because it's possible doesn't necessarily mean it's (highly) probable.
3. Understand the odds in any game you engage yourself, especially if you want to increase the odds of having your desired possibility occur.
4. **Action Item:** Every envisioned outcome you desire should be accompanied by consistent supporting habits that will increase the likelihood of bringing about this outcome. Plan accordingly.
5. **Action Item:** Do not engage in habits that are unsupportive and reduce the likelihood that your "end in mind" will occur.
6. **Action Item:** Imagine, plan and engage in activities that have high probabilities in favor of the results you desire.

Compare the odds against self-change and you will see before you the futility of trying to change others. Play your game best by making choices that improve your odds of success.
– Coach John S. Nagy

16. Stones

Your approach determines much. – *Coach John S. Nagy*

If you're alive, you've probably encountered stones in your road and looked at them as obstacles. From youngsters to old-timers, cultured or unsophisticated, the influence of these stones is felt by all. It doesn't matter who you are or what you do. They're forever present in our lives.

Interestingly, despite the abundance of stones before them, many people don't even see their stones. I only became aware of the stones in my own life a few years back. Before then, stones were not obvious to me because I had (unconsciously) chosen a point of view that tended to overlook any stones in my path. I never learned to look at stones in the ways I could have. It was not a fault on my part. Stones tend to be very quiet about teaching such things.

One such stone I have come to recognize was the inability I had to communicate effectively with others. Because of this particular stone, I stumbled in relationships both professionally and personally. I allowed this stone to get in my way and as a result, I had more failures than I want to admit. Once I finally chose to recognize this stone in a new light, and I came to see it as an opportunity rather than impedance, things started changing swiftly. I chose to step up on my stone rather than be tripped up by it. The opportunity for me to do this was there all along and I eventually took advantage of the lesson my stone was teaching me. By doing this, I learned better communication skills and reaped the rewards of adding that investment to my skill set. I have come to recognize that this stone was just one of many stones present in my life and that other stones were also ready to be acted on.

Now that I've learned to see my stones in a new light, when I look back over the years I've come to truly appreciate the stones I've encountered, both in my own life and in the lives of others. It has been fun learning the influence stones have on us. More importantly, it's fun to see what we can learn from them. I had no idea how much enjoyment and achievement stones could add to life. I wish I had known to look for them sooner. I think they might have made a significant difference earlier in my life.

Some people value their stones and some people don't. Those who do, look forward to dealing with their stones so they can learn more about themselves. Those who don't value their stones often dread them. They look at them as burdens and they often blame others for their "rocky" existence. People who get the most benefit from stones use them to create things – beautiful monuments sometimes, viable institutions at other times. They never fail to see stones as containing opportunities to add value to their lives and to the lives of others.

The people who are least benefited by their stones use them to destroy things – businesses, organizations, and even lives. These people never fail to use their stones. Their focus however is toward offloading them at their first opportunity, because they have not recognized any possible positive impact the stones could have had.

Interestingly enough, the less value people place on their stones, the more the stones seem to get in their way, while the more people value them, the more the stones seem to support them in their adventures. Very curious, these stones are.

Do you have a clue as to what these stones are or (BIG HINT) have I placed a stone in your path?

I see humor and knowledge of human nature in the ancients who invented our language. They really knew what they were describing when they constructed the word "problem." The word comes from the same root as "ballistic" and "Diablo," all of which derive from the root "throw." (An interesting side note: *The word "Diablo" is also related to the words "devil" and "diabolical" and is the root of the saying "The devil is in the details."*) The word "Problem" means "something that is thrown forth, something that gets in the way," like a stone in the path.

From the perspective of the person looking for a smooth path, what is "thrown forth" in his or her path might make for a bumpier ride. Yet that same stone, thrown into a stream, becomes a stepping-stone, making it easier to cross.

It's been some time since I reshaped my attitude toward the stones in my life. I don't mind picking up a few along the path now and then. I never know when a situation I encounter will need just the right stone. I've learned that the very stone that trips up one traveler becomes a stepping-stone in the life of another. A stone that causes one person to sink and drown is exactly what another person need for a toehold to keep his or her head above water. The stones that prevent a garden from being planted often become the border for another garden, a supporting barrier for the well that waters that garden, and the foundation for a building that will store the harvest from that garden. They are not just stones; they are possibilities.

I used to be one of those people who avoided stones. They did not avoid me though; I kept finding that no matter where I turned, somehow a stone would be there to trip me up. I finally realized that *the difference between viewing a stone as a stumbling stone or a stepping-stone is the level at which I provoke my approach to it.*

Provoking Success! (Coach's Review, Recommendations, Questions and Unreasonable Requests)

1. All stones are identical in make-up.

2. Stepping-stones support us.

3. Stumbling stones trip us up.

4. Our own action level determines their impact. In other words, all stones can be for stepping or for stumbling, depending on how we choose to approach each stone.

5. Recognize and *get to know* the stones you have.

6. What can you learn from each stone? You might find a need to share your stone discoveries with someone else in order to learn how they would deal with it. (Do you remember about learning how to advance and improve at playing Pacman?)

7. **Action Item:** Write down your stones into these two categories, stumbling stones and stepping-stones.

8. What have you done or what could you do to approach the stumbling stones on your list at a level that would help you in your journey?

9. **Action Item:** For those stones that haven't been supportive to you, try raising the level of your approach to those stones.

Struggles are but challenges or opportunities in disguise.
– Coach John S. Nagy

Uncommon Time Management

Time manages us. Understand this and your priorities become a lot clearer. — Coach John S. Nagy

17. Beginnings

Life hands us more opportunities to practice effectiveness than we could ever imagine or expect. – Coach John S. Nagy

One day I arrived five minutes late for a workshop I was to attend. This is not a good thing to do when the topic of discussion is "Time Management"!

I didn't have time to realize fully the humor in the situation though. That changed soon after I walked into the room. The facilitator stopped what he was saying to the group. He immediately greeted me with a loud "HELLOOO SON! Glad you could make it. What's your name?"

I froze embarrassed on the spot and experiencing in full what I had heard about deer being caught in headlights. Nervously I responded with my name followed by a very shaky "sir." He smiled like a hungry man who's just been served a two-pound sirloin steak with all the trimmings. "Son, we're just finishing up some warm-up exercises and if the group wouldn't mind, I'd like to include you in it just to wrap it up." He motioned to the group for approval and everyone in the group responded in an affirmative din. He turned back to me and said, "We were all sharing our most special fantasies, and before we can move on to the next lesson, we would like you to share yours with us."

Not realizing that this was a setup to prove a point about arriving on time, I panicked. My mind went absolutely blank. Bad enough that I walked in late; to be put on the "hot seat" so quickly was not what I expected nor wanted.

The room was quiet—too quiet. The deafening sound of my blood rushing through my ears was interrupted only by the echo of my "gulp" coming off the back wall of the auditorium, followed by the giggles coming from the group. My mind raced to assist. Was this a joke? Could he be serious? I smiled nervously, looking for a reality check, "Are you sure you have the time to hold this up?"

"Go ahead son, we're waiting." He looked confident. I guessed that he wasn't joking.

In a word, the stress I was experiencing was "glorious"!

"Sir, my mom told me there would be days like this." I paused & hung my head. "But in the best interests of the class, I'll do it!"

The instructor blinked and I noticed his smile had suddenly gone thin. He looked a bit pale and his forehead began glistening. He started to say that it wasn't necessary and I interrupted, and said I wanted to make good, that he had a right to be upset with my tardiness. I commented that I had walked in late and had held up the group long enough. Moreover, if I had missed the beginning, I was grateful for the opportunity to contribute what I can.

Not thinking anything more about it, I continued. "I'd say that out of all the special thoughts, dreams and fantasies I'd ever had right up to this very moment, the one most desired by me right now is to make it passionately with..." and I paused.

The room was tense with anticipation (or was it dread?). The facilitator's face went red and his movements grew jerky. At that moment, it sank in and I realized "this whole exchange had been a set up to embarrass me for being late. The change in direction had thrown him and now *he* was the one who was embarrassed."

Feeling delight, I shifted gears and kicked into overdrive. I was going to make this count and continued, "...to make it passionately with little or no further embarrassment to that empty chair in the back row, and as quickly as possible."

It took the group five minutes to collect itself. The facilitator himself sat down to catch his breath. This was very good for me since during the collective chaos I got the chance to follow through on my special fantasy. I quietly grinned as I leaned back in my newfound seat.

The facilitator soon put the workshop back on track. He smiled and commented that in the fifteen years he'd been doing that set-up, never before had it turned out like this. With the admittedly unusual opening concluded, he got into the guts of the topic. A most enjoyable presentation it was.

A funny thing though... and for the life of me, I can't understand it. As much as I tried to contribute, even though that instructor knew my name, he never *once* called on me during the rest of that workshop. *I wonder what might have provoked him to avoid me.*

Provoking Success! (Coach's Review, Recommendations, Questions and Unreasonable Requests)

1. **Action Item:** Practice the topic of the day even before you're expected to.
2. **Action Item:** Take only some requests as legitimate.
3. If you're fortunate, expect to be put on the spot for not following through on commitments.
4. Even if you're given an excellent opportunity to show someone up, be kind anyway. You know…."Do unto others..."

Coach's Note: *Getting caught not practicing what you intend to practice and smarting off can get you put into the back row with little opportunity to contribute.*

When you get the spotlight, you've most likely earned it for one reason or another. – Coach John S. Nagy

18. Perfecting Your 'Pre-crastination'

Maybe you should read this tomorrow. – Coach John S. Nagy

You probably noticed that I used the word "Pre-crastination" in
the title of this chapter. No. I didn't misspell this word. I create
it because I needed a word to convey a concept. The word
"procrastination" means "to put off till tomorrow." Since
tomorrow, by definition, never comes, that which is put off never
gets done. Can you relate? The word "Pre-crastination" means,
"To do before tomorrow." Wow! What a novel idea! That's the
premise of this chapter.

An interesting thing occurs when a person finally decides to "get
their act together." It may be that:

- the stress gets too much to handle
- the workload becomes unbearable
- things are not getting done and the company is suffering,
  along with the person responsible

One of the first complaints I hear as a coach is that there just isn't
enough time to do everything that needs to be done. When I
bring up the topic of time management, I hear lots of moans and
groans about not being able to draw up a schedule, much less
stick to one.

Most people would agree that schedules are a fine thing "to have
and to stick to" in the interest of time management. The effective
professional, however, finds more important things to focus on
that have greater impact, if done honestly and thoroughly. Those
more important things are what this chapter covers.

We could be sidetracked into talking about setting priorities, or
examining mission statements, or establishing roles. These items
might be helpful if the focus of this chapter was on time

management. It's not. Our focus is on pre-crastination, which pre-supposes that you already know what your priorities, mission, and roles are. Pre-crastination focuses on getting the things done that need to be done, without interruption. Without exception, these actions require discipline.

The first discipline a person must learn is to account for their time so they can see how it's being spent. This is often a painful experience, because an accurate accounting often reveals significant waste. Who wants to recognize that or to account for that waste of time with someone else? The simple fact is most people don't make it through the first day tracking their use of time. After a very short time, they see what's involved or mush worse, *what it reveals* and they give up —quit! They never make it past this stage.

If this is your challenge, *you can make it past the first stage* and here's how: First, understand going in that you are going to see things that you are not going to like *and that ignoring it does not make it go away.* Second, track your time over fifteen-minute periods throughout the course of a typical week. For those of you who have varied schedules with tremendous sweeps of differing activities, merely log in what functions you're involved in every hour. Be honest about the time you spend waiting idly or doing things that fill time that are not truly working toward your main objectives.

If you make it through the preliminaries – and there are many who don't – your next steps are to complete two lists: one regarding your creative avoidances and another for your procrastinations.

You might be saying, "Hey, wait Coach! What's this 'creative avoidance thingy' you just through into the mix?" That's a good question to be thinking at this moment. Let's explore this.

Have you ever had something you needed to do and decided it could wait because you found something "less painful" to do? That's creative avoidance. The irony in this is that if you come to find that you've chosen something that's even more painful to do than the first painful activity was, you'll often do that thing you avoided in the first place as being the lesser of two evils. Anything you do that takes you away from the things that most need to be done should be written down on your "creative avoidance" list. This list often includes: 1) organizing and reorganizing, 2) preparing and repairing, and 3) diverting attention from more important items.

Prior to coaching, a number of my clients continually prepared for action yet - because of their awesome creative avoidance skills - never actually followed through. People who practice creative avoidance always have some justification or rationalization that seems right to them at the time. The reality is that these same diversions most always fall short in significance compared to what actually needed to be done.

Let's face it. When it comes to procrastination, many of us are experts. We are very creative in making every excuse possible to avoid tasks that need to be started. We justify, rationalize, and even redirect ourselves to continue the process of putting off what needs to be done. That redirection is what creative avoidances are all about.

Coach's Note: *To sabotage these justifications, rationalizations and redirections, it's important to get reality checks on whether the activity you're presently working on is putting "first things first." If this would help you, collaborate with others – now!*

Let's get back to those lists and clarify the difference between the two: procrastinations are those things you need to do that you're not doing; creative avoidances are those things that you do to keep you from doing those things you need to be doing.

Coach's Note: *Yes, you can make these lists in advance without tracking your time if you know what they are! Many people do and doing so will move you to the next stage. Isn't that great! You didn't even get to procrastinate on this one!*

Recognize your creative avoidances by making a list of them. This will help you to create a list of "red flags" that come up and warn you when you are doing things that are on your "to do" list. Supplementing this list with action plans for you to take when these behaviors come up will also help keep you on track. Yes, do not put off creating these action plans either!

Once you list your creative avoidances, finish your procrastination list—"yes" don't put this off! You have the chance to think out and list those things you really need to do to move yourself forward. A good place to start is to envision yourself having accomplished a goal by a set time. With that vision clearly written down, the next step is to create a list of the tasks required to move you toward that goal.

Coach's Note: *If all this is a "stretch" for you, talk it through with someone who's a good note taker! Collaborate!*

The rest of your mission – should you choose to accept it – is to keep yourself aware of when you're doing things on your creative avoidance list that prevent you from doing the things on your procrastination list. "To do" lists, like these, help tremendously (along with some outside feedback, which may include partners, managers, coworkers, spouses, coaches and/or friends). Please pick someone who is willing and able to help you hold yourself accountable for keeping you on your success track. Empower him or her with the authority needed to carry out the responsibility given! This genuine support can be extremely provoking to your efforts to pre-crastinate.

Provoking Success! (Coach's Review, Recommendations, Questions and Unreasonable Requests)

1. Admit that you could make better use of your time than you presently do.

2. **Action Item:** Log your current time usage – be honest!

3. **Action Item:** List your creative avoidances and when done, list your procrastinations.

4. **Action Item:** Create a future vision and create a "To Do List" that supports your vision.

5. **Action Item:** Prioritize your list!

6. Keep vigilant for any activity unsupportive your vision.

7. **Action Item:** Collaborate with someone who can assist you in your process, especially in helping you hold yourself accountable for how you use your time.

8. Helpful "To Do" lists must have realistic deadlines.

9. **Action Item:** Create "mental red flags" that'll alert you to behavior that's ineffective in keeping you on track. Writing them down will implant the flags more deeply in your mind.

10. **Action Item:** Change the name of your procrastination list to "pre-crastination list" and then work your action plans.

11. **Action Item:** Create action plans that will help you get back on track whenever you're not working on what's most important. Don't hesitate! "Kick it into gear" and DO IT!

Coach's Note: *These steps support successes when acted on in a timely manner. There's more to it so provoke yourself to refine your process and add to it as you discover what works best for you.*

There's a direct correlation between deadlines and getting something done; make your deadlines work for you.
– Coach John S. Nagy

19. Got a Moment?

What's your time really worth? If you know, you can let others know. – Coach John S. Nagy

A client and I were talking about what I call "Time Sponges," those daily occurrences that give us nothing in return for our time investment, and actually negatively affect our schedule.

One time sponge is unscheduled interruptions. One client of mine had scheduled her days in five- to ten- minute intervals and when an interruption occurred, it threw everything off track; even a single interruption had a major impact on her operations.

The particular interruption we were discussing that day was typical of interruptions that occur every day in business and in life: an employee sticks her head in the door and asks to speak to you for a "moment." That "moment" can sometimes take up to three hours if you're not well prepared. When schedules are tight, any problems or delays with handling interruptions will trickle-down to create often-significant overall problems. There are many reasons that we have problems with interruptions. Sometimes we get on such familiar terms with our personnel that we become casual about our time boundaries. At other times we're afraid that if we say "no" and request that our time be respected, the interrupter will take offense. Still other times we want our co-workers to think we're there for them, even at our own expense. When you think about it, all of these reasons can get in the way of both good relationships and efficiency of operations.

So let's get a few things understood: You empower someone to interrupt you *when you allow it.* This is especially true in relationships with equals or subordinates. If you don't have the language skill to establish clear limits, people will take advantage of your lack of skill. To avoid on-going time sponges, you need to communicate effectively that it's okay to interrupt you *only long enough to schedule a future time to talk.*

Let's get back to my client's challenge. One of her subordinates periodically came into her office early in the day under the pretense of discussing a legitimate problem. Once engaged, the conversation would digress to other areas, typically eating up two to three hours of time. Obviously, this use of time put a serious crimp in the schedule flow.

To get the best return for her time as possible, I offered her the same the solution I give my other clients who find themselves trapped in this *major time-waster.*

1. Whenever the interrupting party maneuvers into position (to start sponging your time) establish an instant and maintainable limit as to the amount of time you're willing to give them at that moment.

2. Have the interrupter tell you how soon they need to talk with you.

3. Let the interrupter know that you want to give them enough time and uninterrupted focus to be able to discuss their situation-properly.

4. Let the interrupter know that you can best help them if they first clearly describe the situation and offer solutions they think could resolve the perceived problem.

5. Have the interrupter submit this description and proposed solutions to you in writing before the scheduled meeting.

6. Once you establish these guidelines, provoke yourself to maintain them. No one else will.

Coach's Note: *If you're a parent or teacher, this also has practical application in teaching children 1) to take turns and 2) to be creative in coming up with solutions to their problems themselves.*

Provoking Success! (Coach's Review, Recommendations, Questions and Unreasonable Requests)

1. Be aware of when interruptions are occurring.
2. Be okay with saying "no" to interruptions about problems that can be scheduled later.
3. **Action Item:** Ascertain how soon the talk must occur.
4. **Action Item:** Immediately schedule a time to talk, even if it's just a time to talk about when to schedule the talk.
5. Any person interrupting you must be concise about what the interruption is.
6. All interruptions must be justified.
7. **Action Item:** Allow interruptions only to schedule a time to talk and don't allow digressions.
8. **Action Item:** Make the interrupting party write a concise note or memo outlining the problem and any proposed solutions.
9. **Action Item:** Create a viable action plan that will minimize time distractions if you're dealing with an inconsiderate boss.

It is your responsibility to both establish and maintain time boundaries because it is you who will suffer the consequences if you don't. – Coach John S. Nagy

20. Four Simple Questions

The motive behind my every "question" is the **quest I** *am* **on**.
                                        – Coach John S. Nagy

There's only one thing that's more powerful than a good answer
and that's a good question. Coaches know this. We rely on some
powerful questioning techniques to help our clients get to the
next level. The empowerment from a "series" of questions is
even greater.

Several years ago, I learned a set of questions that help
individuals and groups transform themselves. I've shared these
questions with many people since. I'm interested in what occurs
to people as they answer them. Frequently, it's as if lights go on
behind the eyes of both students and clients alike. The change is
sometimes dramatic – as it was for me. These questions gave me
great clarity and a simple method for my own transformation.
Let's get a look at the questions firsthand:

The first question concerns the *present* and asks, "Where are we
now?" This question is not to be taken literally. It is
metaphorical like all the other questions in this set. If taken
literally you might respond that you are sitting in your office.
That's not the point! Rather, this question requests us to make an
inventory of our current conditions, an assessment of the "here
and now" including our attitudes, resources, behaviors, assets,
liabilities, deficits, threats and opportunities.

The second question deals with the *future*, and asks, "Where do
we want to go?" This question requests us to envision what the
future looks like and feels like and what conditions must be
within us or available to us —attitudes, resources, behaviors,
assets, liabilities, deficits, threats and opportunities — in order to
get there.

The third question relates to the path to be taken and asks, "How are we going to get there?" To be able to answer this question, you must consider the steps necessary to accomplish the outcomes you established in your answer to question two. The answers to question three create both the road map and the required actions along the way. They also address any detours that might occur and give contingencies to handle those detours effectively.

The fourth and last question deals with motivation and asks, "How much do we want to get there?" Without the right answer to this question, the first three questions are moot. If you do not know what's motivating you, you're a set-up for the "Why bother?" syndrome.

Coach's Notes: *It's wise to note that leaving just one of these questions unanswered could cause problems. Here are some questions to ask yourself to help clarify your understanding of the importance of asking all these questions completely.*

1. What would occur if you started on your journey not clearly knowing why? (What's your motivation?)

2. Metaphorically, how would you think the journey might end if you thought you were in Los Angeles and started traveling east toward Chicago, when you were really in Miami when you started? (What's your starting point?)

3. How would things end up for you if you had good road maps and didn't have a clearly thought out destination? (What are your expected results?)

4. What would occur if you knew where you were to start from and where you wanted to end and had no action plan to make the journey possible? (What are your planned actions and path?)

If your responses to these four questions are like those of most people, you should get a clear picture as to why **all** the original questions are asked. To do otherwise invites problems.

Go through the questions for yourself. *Your answers may just provoke you to greater successes.*

I hope the light behind your eyes shines brightly!

Provoking Success! (Coach's Review, Recommendations, Questions and Unreasonable Requests)

1. Questions are "quests" that are presented in words.

2. Where are you now?

3. Where do you want to go/be?

4. How are you going to get there?

5. How much do you want to get there?

6. Know your quests better by becoming able to state them clearly.

7. *Add one final question to your list:* How soon shall you start and then finish each quest?

8. **Action Item:** If you do not have them already, engage yourself in a quest to identify five achievements that would make your life or business better. Put a time limit on each quest. Make sure all other questions are answered to support your quest – including the "how soon?" question.

Start all your quests with at least one great question!
– Coach John S. Nagy

21. Burned Out Yet?

You will never reach the horizon, ever. – *Coach John S. Nagy*

We dreamers, plotters and schemers of the world sometimes don't recognize a basic need to celebrate our victories. Swept up in activities, we tend to "do what needs to be done" or "plan what needs to be done," and we forget some other equally important behaviors – valuing and appreciating what we have before us.

Working and living focusing only on doing some goal or planning for the next goal creates imbalance. Neither the doing nor the planning, if lived exclusively, leaves any time to appreciate what actually has been accomplished: the "results" part of our business and lives.

Continuously pushing that achievement horizon out can devalue and depreciate where we are now. What we have then does not nurture and recharge the resources we expend attempting to get there. Here are some blunt facts: That horizon is always going to be out there beyond your reach. It looks great and offers much promise. It does not nurture you or provide you with anything that will nurture you. It's what you achieve on the journey that does. If you don't recognize and take action on this, you can be left with an unsatisfied feeling that, over time, causes burnout.

I've seen clients do this – work toward their horizon without stopping to celebrate and recharge themselves. They never "enjoy the fruits of their labor!" They live constantly with the focus on where they are now and where they want to be, continually pushing their mental horizon toward new goals and insights. They never enjoy the moment in the "here and now."

It's a hard habit to break. I've created this moving horizon many times in my own life, both professionally and personally. You can guess the results. I have major swings in my energy level and when my energy level is low, it forces me to take time to recharge and get my bearings straight.

I've come to understand that my mental "aspiring" horizon is always going to be moving out ahead. In many respects that old saying "A person's reach should exceed his or her grasp" comes to mind here and it's offered to affirm that the habit of pushing the horizon out is not bad – it just needs to have balance. I've put periodic reminders in place that tell me that I need to take steps to keep my perspective in balance and take time to enjoy the victories of the moment. Savoring an accomplishment is well worth the effort even if I do this only occasionally. The key though is *doing it* occasionally!

Most people in business (and in life) can celebrate, savor, and recharge themselves very effectively by applying a simple formula to their daily routine. Ironically, this formula is based on the very same letters of the word that it needs to fill – the "gap!" The acronym, "GAP" can be used in the evening just before you go to bed or just as you're leaving work. It stands for "Generate, Appreciate and Praise," and goes like this:

G: **Generate** a daily accounting of your wins for that day. Keep a log just for this activity. Do this despite any setbacks. Find something you can come away with that adds value to you and those you involve yourself with professionally and personally. List at least three (3) wins every day, if possible.

A: **Appreciate** the full extent of these wins and start answering the question, "What do those wins mean as part of the progress I'm making toward the goals I've set?" Share the wins with someone who can appreciate them with you. Even if the person may not fully understand what your wins are, or what they mean to you, take time to share the valuing thoughts and energy they engender.

P: **Praise** and honor yourself for the work you did to bring about your accomplishments. You've earned it! If you don't give yourself this respect, over time the value of your efforts diminishes. We're NOT talking about comparing yourself to others and telling yourself you are better than they are because you accomplished your goal. We are talking about comparing yourself to yourself, where you are on your roadmap compared to where you were and to where you might be if you hadn't set and accomplished your goal. The heady rush you once received for doing the job well goes away after a while if you have no pay off. Get your pay off on a daily basis by praising yourself for the hard work you've done and the results you've achieved. (**Coach's Note:** *If you cannot, because of your faith, take credit for that which you've achieved, perhaps you may find this stage more affirming to you if you were to praise the Source of that which you appreciate most. Whatever you care to do here, make sure you are doing it in the most honoring of manners you can.*)

This is important: look at your GAP and fill it every day so the emptiness or burnout that could occur for high-achievers never gets a chance to take root. If you're working on goals with others, imagine the impact of doing this GAP activity with your people at the end of the day! *What successes might your actions provoke in yourself and others?*

Notice what's really going on here. You might be the type of person who continually focuses on that that horizon line. If this is your tendency, it most likely won't change. Appreciate this fact and add some balance. Take the gap that you always create and fill it with sincere appreciation for yourself and for your team. Fill the gap with this GAP activity and add value to the efforts of all involved.

Provoking Success! (Coach's Review, Recommendations, Questions and Unreasonable Requests)

1. Fill your GAP at day's end and get that recharge you deserve and EARNED!
2. The horizon never pays off. You gain from the results of efforts that you put in right now.
3. **Action Item:** Take time to enjoy and celebrate those efforts every day and watch the recharged rush you give yourself and the people around you.
4. Extend this principle to those you work and live with.
5. **Action Item:** Learn what their "wins" are and generate a list of their accomplishments to share with them when you see them succeeding.
6. **Action Item:** Provoke moments to help them appreciate the effect their success is having on them.
7. **Action Item:** Share honest praise with them for their efforts.

Coach's Note: *Practicing this concept in relationships also has the benefit of helping others to remain on track in their work for you because they know they are valued and most people, once they know they can please you and please themselves, too, will want to continue that success.*

The only attraction a horizon can offer you is its beauty; so enjoy the journey toward it since that's all you really have.
– Coach John S. Nagy

22. Running on Empty

Break the hold of your focus when it's not providing you with what you need. – Coach John S. Nagy

The idea that you're "running on empty" might not occur to you until the "powers that be" smack you in the face with the news. Subtle reminders like a slightly sluggish pace and a lessening in the usual bounce in your step or a stressed-filled heartbeat may not drive the point home. If it's our habit to continue running when there's nothing fueling us, we tend to keep going until we're "out of commission" on the side of the road.

Very often, after "running on empty" for some time, things start happening that grab our attention and jar us out of our self-induced complacency about our state. We find:

- personal conflicts occur more often
- our focus or concentration loses its edge
- we lack our usual energy and motivation
- we receive direct assaults on our accustomed way of life, like the car dieing in the middle of traffic

For me, it's generally all of the above, topped with a very bad head cold and an overall feeling of exhaustion that gets the point across to me that I'm not taking care of myself. I'm one who tends to ignore the more casual signs of self-neglect and I need to engage a higher authority to get me to pay attention. Even when the signs and messages occur, my response time is usually in low gear due to the low priority I give to them.

Taking time for "me" is not something I do as often as I tell my clients to do. It's my job to point out what they may not be able to see. They value this appraisal highly - just about as highly as I do when my coach gets on my case (and he does so regularly and with my permission!)

That's my reality at times. When I have all the signs hitting me squarely in the face, including a message from my own coach telling me to take it easy and re-charge those batteries – I listen and take action accordingly.

Well, maybe not so immediately. I'm getting better though. It used to take 10 indicators to provoke my attention. Now I'm down to only one.

How many does it take for you?

Provoking Success! (Coach's Review, Recommendations, Questions and Unreasonable Requests)

1. **Action Item:** Schedule time for yourself and do this *regularly*. Be sure that this time is non-business related.
2. Make sure this time is designed to recharge your personal batteries.
3. **Action Item:** Let everyone know that you are not to be disturbed, no matter what (and "yes" use common sense in emergencies).
4. **Action Item:** Train yourself to think about things other than work or other stressful issues during this time.
5. **Action Item:** Do something you enjoy. Do it alone or with family or friends.
6. Enjoy yourself in a realm that is not professionally related – AT ALL! Remember to take a vacation from your vocation! Get refreshed!

Productivity improves when you maintain your producing machine. – Coach John S. Nagy

23. An Overwhelming Message

If you listen carefully, you may just get it. — *Coach John S. Nagy*

Many people experience it, few of them listen to it and virtually everyone feels it at least occasionally. I'm talking about the commonly occurring emotion of "overwhelm."

You might say "Huh? What's that?" and "What's the coach talking about when he says few people listen to it?"

It's true what I say about many people experiencing the emotion. It's just as true about many people not listening to it. Many business professionals in high-stress positions tend to train themselves to ignore their emotions when it comes to business obligations. They push forward at all costs, often without realizing that those costs can include their own health.

It doesn't have to be that way. Listening carefully to the message this emotion sends (and taking appropriate actions) will always, both to the person feeling overwhelmed and to those around him/her, prove to be more beneficial, than ignoring the message would. In other words, the long-term benefits to be gained from listening (and heeding) the message will always outweigh any short-term gains that might come from ignoring it.

What's the message? The message that this emotion gives is derived from the root history of the word: The word "overwhelm" comes from the nautical root word "whelm" which means to flip over a boat. To "overwhelm" is to go one stage further and to sink the vessel after it's been flipped over.

Keep in mind, as you picture this scenario, what is going on to everyone who is aboard that ship. It's hard to imagine anyone in such a situation having an easy time being able to breathe, or even being able to keep his or her heads above water.

Since we are creating a tangible picture of a situation to show what feeling overwhelmed is like, let's add another element that fits into this picture: The original Latin root of the word "spirit" means breath or "respiration" and is closely related to the word "inspiration." Put the background of the two words – overwhelmed and spirit - together and you make a startling discovery: Every time that you're in the state of feeling overwhelm, picture yourself as being under a capsized ship. What occurs quickly if you're not rescued or you do not manage to extricate yourself? Did you guess, "Your spirit leaves you?" Fortunately for us, we need not sweat (perspire) too much over this. Being overwhelmed is usually not a permanent state. The feeling only lasts just for the time you're submerged. There's a good chance that if you are experiencing what is called (appropriately) having a "sinking feeling," you are experiencing overwhelm.

Things get worse if you're at the point where you feel chronically overwhelmed. You feel as if you can never get your "head above water." Those people fortunate enough to be able to drag themselves out of an overwhelmed condition—with or without assistance – take a long time to catch their breath again. If they're fortunate, and have proper care, eventually their breath will come back to them. (Coaching Exercise: *Go back and substitute the word "spirit" for the word "breath" in this paragraph. Read it again with the substitution and ask yourself if you have ever had your spirit affected like this.*)

If you take the root histories of words like these and apply them to the business world, you'll see why it's important to heed the message they give. If you're experiencing overwhelm, it's time to reassess your situation.

Start by getting in touch with the feelings – body sensations – within you that overwhelm produces. Perhaps feelings likened to being suffocated or drowned by the things that surround you, just as if water surrounds you if you are under a capsized ship. Another way to get the picture is to make note that all our moment to moment abilities to "take things in easily" and "let things go easily"(to "breathe," go with the flow or to feel creatively inspired) are diminished to the point that if these functions are operating at all, they're barely discernable. Those "things" we can no longer "take in" or "let go" include any tasks, ideas, emotions, energy, demands upon us from others, and may even include any situation with which you're involved.

You might say, "Great, Coach. Now that I can identify that my boat has flipped over and is sinking, I can't breathe, and I'm having a hard time trying to come up for air, how do all these root word histories help me?"

I'm glad you asked.

Overwhelm occurs when one or more of two extreme conditions take place. The first condition occurs when putting out to sail in a vessel that's excessively small to operate successfully in the existing conditions at sea. The second condition occurs when putting out to sail in a vessel that is carrying entirely too much on board to maintain buoyancy. In either case, the first storm will overwhelm the boat and cause it to sink. Maybe this will only take a ripple – just like the proverbial "straw that broke the camel's back. In real life, overwhelm occurs when you start your journey with too many things "on board." You don't plan on any changing sea conditions. You're sunk when you find you're too heavily burdened to even deal with minor ripples. When the first wave hits, water comes over the helm and starts the process of submersion. That's when your breathing difficulties begin.

How do you get yourself out of this situation? The first thing to do is recognize that you're in it. The next step is to start letting go of those things that are holding you under and preventing you from breathing. Remember, it's usually a combination of the roughness of the sea and the weight of the "things" on board which creates your desperate need for air to breathe. Only by recognizing the major contributors to the condition you're in can you change it and move away from their influence.

Of course, the best way to get out of the situation is to prevent it in the first place. Know your limits and honor them before you start your journey. Say "no" when you need to say "no." To take on more than you can handle is not heroic; it's provoking yourself toward inundation, overwhelm and ultimately failure. *Provoke yourself toward breathing easier and better!*

Provoking Success! (Coach's Review, Recommendations, Questions and Unreasonable Requests)

1. Recognize what your personal "overwhelm indicators" are and write them down.

2. **Action Item:** Assess all contributing factors to "overwhelmed" and write them down.

3. **Action Item:** Ask yourself what's most important – with health being your top priority.

4. **Action Item:** Start the process of letting go of those things that inundate you.

5. **Action Item:** Provoke yourself toward things that nurture your well-being and that allow you to breathe more easily in all your activities.

Breathing is not just a physical process; it's essential for good business and a good life. – Coach John S. Nagy

24. Invest Now or Pay Dearly Later

Some people and companies specialize in training at high cost rather than producing at low cost. It's no wonder they never improve their businesses or their lives. – Coach John S. Nagy

Have you ever been in a position where one or more key employees left your employment and you had no clue as to what they did or how they did it? On the other hand, perhaps you're one of the few bosses who actually know the tasks assigned to your employees and how to do each task. You may even have a list of all their tasks and the processes required to perform these tasks clearly laid out in your mind. In exceptional cases, you might even know the timing of all these "to do's" and can readily communicate this schedule when asked.

If these latter situations are what you have going for you, I applaud you. If not, think about the following: What position will you be in if your employees quit (or perhaps get sick, are injured or die), leave no written record of what their routines are, and how they are to be done? Does this thought disturb you in any way? If your more likely to train others by showing them how to and when to do things, you've actually created a problem. If they leave, you're going to have to dedicate that same amount of time, energy, money and spirit – directly or indirectly – into training the new employees who come onboard to replace them.

If you have employees, this is not good news. As an employer, there's a good probability that your staff won't be around someday when you need them most – leaving you to figure out what they did and how they did it before you can begin to train their replacements.

Let's face it: this occurs often enough that it has become accepted as a necessary cost of doing business. What a shame, when you could simply add one key element to normal business processes that would spare your organization this enormous drainage of resources.

"Coach!" you might say, "Don't leave us hanging. What could that key be?"

I'm glad you asked. That missing element is 'documentation' in the form of a procedures manual. It can't get much simpler than that.

With proper documentation, you prevent having to re-invest yourself in training replacements when they arrive on your doorstep. If you've not documented all the "what, when, where, why and how aspects of each position in your business, then you have to re-invest yourself each time and for each newbie in the tedious job of training them before you can bring them up to speed on operations. Count on it. This will occur every time you have a new employee show up if you don't already have the process down on paper.

Let's up the ante one more chip. What happens if the new employee leaves in mid-training? What occurs if you have to hire a "temp" while you're searching for the next replacement? What are you prepared to do? Can you afford the resource draining elements required to do training *and* keep your operations functioning smoothly?

"But Coach!" you might protest, "I've already got a system up and running and I don't have any time I can dedicate to this kind of activity. It would take up too much of my time."

I agree! I also see that the course you've laid out for yourself means that you'll have to interrupt your operations to "make time" for when the unanticipated occurs.

Tough talk eh? Let me ask you some questions. Are you open and available to learn a different way of operating? Do you want to put your operation in a favorable position so that when transitions occur, they have a negligible impact on you and your business? Are you open to a process that you can participate in willingly and on your own terms that will help your operations in the future?

I'm hoping you're saying to all of this "Yes, Coach! Absolutely." If you are, then I say *"Great! I have some suggestions to make your investment in new hires pay off sooner and even better!"*

There is a technique you can use if you want a more systematic, "turn-key ready" business operation. If you practice it diligently, you'll reap tremendous rewards. This technique is especially beneficial to those individuals who already have a business up and running and don't have time to write down all the "how-to's" that are dictated by many "turnkey ready" philosophies. If a concerted effort is made at the right time, this technique will save the typical business owner many times the time and money that he/she would normally use in training new hires.

Before I describe the technique, let me share the benefits with you so you know that it's in your best interest to keep reading! In any business, the "end-in-mind" is an operation that produces income in as effortless a manner as possible for the person who owns and operates it. Let's face it, if you have to spend inordinate and unnecessary time training your employees, then you're not running a business, *you're running a school and you're paying the students to boot!*

The number one benefit you can expect to reap from implementing a "pre-emptive" technique is to keep your processes flowing more smoothly when anything unanticipated occurs. This will mean fewer training hassles and expenses, fewer process interruptions and snags, and less waste of time and expense for you and for any others involved in the training process.

Let's walk through a typical situation: One day, "Connie," your purchasing agent, quits when she becomes pregnant. Connie was a jewel; unfortunately, she took all that jewel-like knowledge of sellers and procedures with her when she walked out the door. Now you, as owner/operator, must hire and train her replacement "Ralph" to do the functions Connie did. This requires much time, patience and effort on the part of the company, with no guarantee that Ralph will receive all the information required to be an effective purchasing agent. To make things worse, you may have no idea "how" Connie did her magic; you only saw her results. You must now face learning both "how" Connie did her job **and** trying to "teach" it to Ralph – effectively "re-inventing the wheel."

When a situation like this occurs, you now have an opportunity to use the replacement's very unfamiliarity with the job to clarify your process. Here's how.

Your "end in mind" should be …

- A procedure that is fully understood by the employee

- A reality check of your own understanding or the trainer's understanding of the process

- A reality check on how well you or the trainer can communicate this process by having new employees write down the process—if they can't, you have a weak link!

- The finished writing of the processes is now a reference document for future use

- A link or page in a "procedures manual" for that particular function

- Decreases in time, effort, and money spent on training

- Delegation of documentation tasks (as much as possible) to someone else freeing your time for more pressing matters

With these ends in mind, here's a simple way to get there.

1. Share "1) through 6)" of the "end-in-mind" goal list with the new employee. The employee should understand what is expected of them.
2. Explain that the employee will be responsible for documenting what they have learned.
3. As the employee learns the process, have him document each step.
4. Review the process description.
5. Make whatever adjustments or modifications are necessary
6. Review the adjustments with the employee.
7. Once the training is completed, have the employee write or type up the process legibly and in enough detail that future employees would have a full understanding of the job requirements. (Yes, this may require an assist from a typist in some cases.)
8. Have the employee make a duplicate copy of the document to store in a place convenient to you and any others who might need access to it as a file for future reference and revision.

Points to Ponder: This whole process can be performed by:

- You as the trainer of a new employee
- You as the trainer of a current employee
- Another employee as the trainer of a new or current employee

- you as the trainer with you as the current employee (You might want to share your documentation with a coach or someone who can check to see if you unknowing left out any short cuts or other important information that is so obvious and well known to you that you didn't write it down).

Additional Points to Ponder: Timing is everything!

- Make sure that you include *when* the procedure needs to be performed.
- Add to the document any tasks that need to be done before the actual procedure can take place.
- Add any "next step" activities that should be anticipated or started when the procedure is completed.

Those of us who embrace the "work smarter-not harder" business practice philosophy and currently have businesses may find it difficult to go back and document the enormous machine that we've created. Following procedures like these provokes us through the tedious documentation process and brings about a smoother and less costly flow in our future.

Here's a quick story of reference: A dear client of mine used this recommendation and had the assistance of a "gem" of an employee. The employee volunteered to get a procedures manual written within two weeks – she had it done in five days (I did mention she was a gem didn't I?). Twenty-five days later, that employee unexpectedly quit due to a health problem. Her health problem prevented her from being available to train her replacement. Because my client provoked the creation of the manual, she was able to hire and train the replacement in record time. That investment in creating the manual not 30 days before provoked much savings of time, money and energy.

Provoking Success! (Coach's Review, Recommendations, Questions and Unreasonable Requests)

1. Recognize the need for preventive action.

2. Be proactive and not reactive when things are so hectic that you're taking action in "survival" mode. Why? Look at the "Overwhelming" chapter for clues!

3. **Action Item:** Seek and anticipate opportunities that empower you to prevent future time sponges.

4. **Action Item:** Repeat pro-activity as needed to keep your business positioned favorably when the unanticipated does occur.

5. Keep in mind that this concept works in private "non business" matters just as well. (*Examples*: Have you ever wished you had something written out for you explaining what you have to do, like laundry, cooking, or recording a TV show, when your significant other is not at home? Have you ever been part of a civic association board of directors that ran the organization in an "ad hoc" manner because no one documented what needed to be done or how to do it?)

The goal is not to hire and train; it is to produce.
— Coach John S. Nagy

Uncommon Planning
and Review

Continually review your results (your present situation) and then project ahead. – Coach John S. Nagy

25. What's Your Choice?

How you attend to things is all a matter of investment.
                                        – Coach John S. Nagy

In a few of the classes I teach, I start out with a question so simple it doesn't seem to demand much thought. When answered, it sets the direction of the class in a universally beneficial way. The question is straightforward and has to do with how each person chooses to attend the class. I preface the question with three options, one of which the student must choose when they give their answer.

The first of the three options is the simplest and requires the least commitment. In coaching terms, it merely requires the person to sit in the grandstand and observe. Hence, the first option is to be an observer. The "observer" choice allows for an occasional cheer or two by the attendee directed toward the people who are on the playing field. A few notes may be taken regarding what's going on in the game. The person choosing to observe invests the minimum amount possible. They are not in the game, only watching it from afar.

The second choice requires a bit more commitment from the person who selects it. I liken it to being on the sidelines, where, you may be called, at a moment's notice, into the game for a play or two. As soon as the play is over, you are immediately sidelined again until you're called back into the game. This level of commitment requires a certain readiness to be able to participate actively on very short notice. Hence, the choice the person makes is to be a participant only. The drawback in this choice is that the game-play is "hit or miss" and only requires a response when necessary. Otherwise, the participant is active only when called upon. Most of the time is spent waiting for a chance to play.

The final choice is the one that requires the most commitment from the attendee; It's equivalent to being in the game all the time, fighting with all your might not to be sidelined, and being fully committed to the outcome. The person who takes this option knows the rules very well and may have even written some of them. Their investment is total and they know what's required to play and win.

Since the game is big, all participants know that other participants are involved. To stay in the game, you must contribute something of value. When you choose to be a contributor, you receive maximum returns on those contributions.

At this point, I add a "stinger" to the class discussion. I let them know that if they choose to play at the highest level, they must be willing to put something on the line that they may lose if they do not perform at their peak during class. The criteria are straightforward. I let them know what they will win and how they can win it. I also let them know what will occur if they do not perform as they've promised.

An interesting thing occurs in these discussions: the process that unfolds in class is precisely that which occurs in life. The attendees understand very clearly that if they wish to get anything worthwhile out of the class – and out of life – their obvious response is the one that provokes the most commitment and follow through.

When I finally ask the provoking "How each person wishes to attend the class" question, it's a rare instance when I have anyone who wishes to attend at anything other than the highest level. With such an opportunity, choosing anything less just wouldn't make any sense.

Provoking Success! (Coach's Review, Recommendations, Questions and Unreasonable Requests)

1. How do you plan on attending? As an observer? A participant? Or as a contributor?

2. What have you been giving up because of nonperformance? **Action Item:** Make a list.

3. What are you willing to put on the line? What is your actual investment? **Action Item:** Make a list.

4. **Action Item:** Make a list of what it is that you want to win. What does each win look and feel like to you?

5. **Action Item:** Make a list of what you're willing to let go in your life due to nonperformance.

6. What's YOUR choice?

7. **Action Item:** Make a list of choices that you could make better in the future. How do you see those choices playing out? Create a vision of what that looks like if the better choice is made.

Those most involved reap the most reward.
– Coach John S. Nagy

26. Back to Basics

Coach Nagy's 11th Commandment: "Honor thyself."

Let's suspend disbelief for a few moments and imagine that you are about to close out this year and reboot into a new one. You may want to take a moment to start this "new year "with a stronger personal foundation. If so, here's my gift to you, an end-of-the-year bonus.

So that you understand the importance of this gift I am offering, ask yourself:

1. How would you feel if you had upfront and personal validation, coming to you constantly?
2. How would you feel if you knew that just by hanging around for the last 365 days you'd made a valuable difference?
3. How would you feel if you knew beyond any doubt that your world was moving in the right direction?

These are serious questions and I hope you're taking the time to explore them. They may seem rhetorical in nature if you feel tempted to respond immediately to them by saying, "Who's going to say 'no'?" If you inspect the questions again you will see that they are not "yes" or "no" or one word answer (like "good," "great" or "wonderful") questions. They are energy queries – created to "provoke" you (successfully, I hope!) to invest in your "self." Part of this investment involves connecting yourself with the energies these questions are asking you to explore. *They require you to get "out of your head" and "into your heart."*

If you haven't done so, please provoke yourself to invest the time to truly reflect and respond to them. *Aren't you worth it?*

Have you finished yet? Good. Let's continue exploring.

Something missing from the daily routines of most people is the simple act of reflection. When done and done well, reflection lets us know that we are on a journey with many lessons – some learned easily, some not. When done poorly, reflection will both hold us back and drain the life out of us. Poor reflection doesn't provide us with vital feedback needed to improve both our performance and the conditions before us. Poor reflection degrades our choices making them both ineffective and inefficient. Because of poor reflection, often times the same lessons must occur repeatedly until we do learn what we need to learn. This too is very draining and unsupportive of success.

Provoke success for yourself by taking a good look at your own practice of reflection and get it down right so that your next year actions provide strong support for the person you choose to be.

The request I put to you is simple. It'll take only a few moments and can continue over the course of a several days. It requires only a pad of paper, a pen or pencil and a commitment to see it through to completion. Start by numbering the left-side column on the first two sheets starting with the number one and proceeding consecutively as high as the pages will allow you. The typical letter page will hold about 25 rows.

Now focus on all the wins, successes, and fulfilling things you did over this last year. Yes! I'm serious here. Every time you think of something that brought you joy, contentment and fulfillment during this last year that was the direct result of your activities, write that item down on your list. If you answered those three questions asked of you earlier in this chapter, then you already know what to expect as a return on your investment here.

Provoking Success! (Coach's Review, Recommendations, Questions and Unreasonable Requests)

1. **Action Item:** Ask yourself how you would feel having a pat on the back for making a valuable, significant difference for yourself during the past year.

2. **Action Item:** List all the valuable, significant differences you've made for yourself over that past year. Include all your wins, successes, and fulfillments.

3. **Action Item:** Give yourself a pat on the back and a big hug for moving forward in your life. If you don't believe you're worth it, who else will?

Coach's Bonus Activity: *Create another list of all the valuable contributions you've made to others. Anything and everything that benefit another person's being should be written on that list.*

For those of you having a hard time coming up with things to put on your list, consider this: 365 days represents 8,760 hours or 525,600 minutes. If you can't come up with at least a few wins, successes, and fulfilling things to write down, you'll definitely be interested in the next chapter.

Above all, know what a 'win' is for you. Play your game and make sure you have strong evidence that you're winning!
– Coach John S. Nagy

27. So! What's Next?

*Ends-in-mind (what you ultimately want to accomplish) are
annoying little reminders of what our true intentions are.*
— Coach John S. Nagy

Coach Note: *This chapter could be considered a continuation of
the "Back to Basics" chapter. I hope that you took that chapter's
challenge and you're ready to take this next one too. If not,
please consider investing the time to work through the last
chapter, before you continue with this one, so you may get the
maximum benefit this current chapter has to offer.*

My coach asked me to do something one year that, in retrospect,
made quite a difference for me: During one of my first coaching
sessions of the year with him, he asked me to make a list of 100
things I wanted to accomplish during the upcoming year.

He told me that everything on the list had to be in-line with my
purpose and it had to make a difference for myself (and possibly
others.)

I took action on his request. Everything I could think of went
onto that list. I listed:

- odd jobs I wanted to do around the house
- items that needed to be put to rest
- gardening activities
- touch-up jobs
- projects that I had been thinking about and never gotten
  around to
- general cleanup activities that would make a big difference
  in the overall appearance of my home

I added to my list:

- activities I wanted to experience with my family
- things, that through my actions, I wanted my family to have
- words I wanted to share that I had not said yet

I continued to list more things as I ventured into the business areas of my life. I wrote down:

- growth goals
- marketing projects
- campaigns
- value-added items I wanted my clients to receive from their experience of being coached by me

When I was done writing, I had come up with well over 100 things. I looked at my list and thought, "How am I going to get all this stuff done?" That's exactly what I asked my coach. He smiled and said, "That's where project planning and time management come into play."

I'm delighted to report to you that one year later, 95 percent of the items on my list were completed. The remaining few items were well on their way to being completed within forty-five days. I'd say that the greatest satisfaction for me in all of this was being able to look at my list of "completions." I was getting things done that were making a difference for me and for others. What a great feeling! *And I provoked it!*

What about you? Are you ready to provoke yourself toward a purposeful life? Great! Here's what to do:

Provoking Success! (Coach's Review, Recommendations, Questions and Unreasonable Requests)

1. Think about all the things you'd like to accomplish (on-purpose) over the next year.

2. **Action Item:** Write them down on a sheet of paper. Shoot for at least 100 items (two items per week over the next year with two weeks off to just "be.")

3. **Action Item:** Pick one or two items that you know you can accomplish quickly and completely.

4. **Action Item:** Create a folder for each project and place both of them on your scheduled "to do's."

5. **Action Item:** Complete them *as scheduled.*

6. **Action Item:** Repeat steps three through six until all the items on your list are completed.

Coach's Bonus Activity: *Feel free to add any items to your list that come up during the year if they are in the spirit of what you envisioned your year to be and they support your focus. Make sure, though, that you give yourself the same time that you did the items on your original list.* In other words, don't give yourself a massive project on the 364th day and expect yourself to have it finished overnight.

Have a Bodacious Year!

Keeping track with an accurate scoreboard is a great way to be sure you're winning. – Coach John S. Nagy

28. Control Issues Made Easy

Understanding and applying the basics of control empowers all.
        – Coach John S. Nagy

Many of my clients and students truly desire to have more control
in their lives. They express this almost every time they get into a
coaching conversation with me, either as a direct request, or as a
subtler less direct wish that I pick up during our talks. Because
of repeated requests, I've come up with a very easy way to
explain what is involved with "control." Most of my clients
appreciate hearing this explanation and I hope your experience
will be the same.

Control is a very simple process to understand. It has three key
components:

- The first component relates to knowing what you ultimately
  want.
- The second component deals with your ability to perceive
  reality clearly.
- The last component has to do with your ability to make
  choices and take action based on your choices.

The first component reflects the vision you have of the future.
This vision leads you forward. You have a clear picture, feeling,
or vision of what you want the outcome to be and you experience
your vision as the desired results and consequences of well-
coordinated choices and actions. In "Stephen Covey" terms, it is
your "end-in-mind."

The second component reflects how well you are able to perceive
the differences between "what is" (your present reality) and
"what should be" (your future vision). It includes everything a
person needs in order to monitor the "here and now," while
continuing to maintain awareness of the direction the current

settings will take you. In management terms, this is your supervising and feedback function.

The last component reflects your ability to be proactive, to take appropriate action, whenever necessary, and to adjust the process so you will achieve your desired outcome. It is also a test of how well you make choices and follow-through on them to achieve satisfactory results.

A good way to illustrate this process is to imagine being the driver of a car and having some destination in mind.

The first component consists of keeping in mind how your car should be traveling toward your desired destination. As you monitor your travels, you may discover that your vehicle is traveling too fast or too slow. It may be that your vehicle is veering too much to the left or right. No matter what your observations may be, the next choice on your part is to make adjustments as necessary to bring your vehicle back onto the track that will get you to your destination and get you there in one piece. These minor adjustments make it possible for you to direct your vehicle to its intended goal within the intended guidelines of the intended path.

Control is the process of monitoring one's performance and taking appropriate actions to get desired results. It's simple. If you're unable to do this, you're not in control.

Problems that occur for individuals who are attempting to get control back into their lives always relate to one of these three components:

1. *Lack of clear focus regarding the desired results* – A person must have a clear picture of what is wanted – that *end-in-mind.* It makes a difference in both the actions taken and

how closely monitored the process is to obtain the outcome sought.

2. *Inability to see reality clearly and accurately* - A person must be able to see reality clearly and continue to make accurate observations about what is occurring in the here-and-now. Clarity of the end-in-mind makes a significant difference for the choices made.

3. *Inabilities to proactively choose and act accordingly* - A person must be able to respond appropriately to current conditions to adjust actions to support the end-in-mind. Problems occur when a person is unable to project into the future the impact of current conditions and choices.

When two or more people are involved in the control process, problems that can occur, usually relate to how each individual involved in the process is operating. If anyone involved in the process is unable to understand and implement the three necessary components presented above, his or her operation within the control process will suffer. Once their operation suffers, he or she will be unable to operate "together or with" others. Another way of saying this is the person will be unable to "co-operate."

Life' is difficult enough to get a handle on without having to get involved in control issues. Most of the "control issues" I hear my clients complain about concerning people they work (or live) with are actually "directing" issues more than anything else. The end-in-mind is clear and so is the ability to see what is going on. The choices and the ability to respond are often where the causes of disagreement occur. This may include subtle differences in what each party wants as the outcome.

My usual observations in such matters are that there's a need to put one or more of the three components back into the process. This includes working things out with the people with whom we choose to cooperate. If they are not in control, it is impossible to expect them to co-operate with us.

This thought leads us to other questions:

- With whom do we choose to partner?
- What provoked us to choose them?
- How long do we choose to stay in situations when it's clear that co-operation is impossible?
- Why do we stay?

Provoking Success! (Coach's Review, Recommendations, Questions and Unreasonable Requests)

1. **Action Item:** Clarify what the outcome(s) should be.
2. **Action Item:** Clarify your guidelines.
3. **Action Item:** Clarify what adjustments can and can't be made.
4. **Action Item:** Keep your eyes peeled to monitor progress.
5. **Action Item:** Make adjustments according to the guidelines you have established.
6. **Action Item:** Control is not an event; it is a process. Provoke yourself toward partnerships supportive of yours.

Coach's Bonus Activity: *Choose to deal only with people who can do the above and avoid interactions with people who can't.*

Trying to work with people who are reactive, misguided and unmanageable is like trying to herd cats. All you'll accomplish is annoyance of yourself and the cats. – Coach John S. Nagy

29. The Cost of Nonperformance

*If you knew up-front what it was you were walking away from,
you might stick around a bit longer. — Coach John S. Nagy*

Often it's what we refuse to see that costs us the most. While I
was teaching a goal-setting class the other day, someone asked
me a question. The interesting thing about it is that the person
asking the question already knew the answer she needed.
Unfortunately, she was fishing for information that, had I given it
to her, would have diverted her from realizing it for herself.
Giving her the answer might even have caused her much lost
time. Her question related to recommendations she wanted me to
make about books she could read that would be motivational for
her. She believed that she could have achieved much more in her
life had she been able to stay more motivated. She also knew she
was challenged in that area of her life.

As a facilitator and fellow human being, I did not see it as my
place to agree or disagree with her. I learned early on that most
people are usually very motivated, even when they say they
aren't. You can see the truth of this in how people choose to
invest in themselves. If you look at how people occupy their
time, you'll see what they're motivated toward doing.

This includes many individuals who spend their time, day in and
day out, in mindless or fruitless activities. You might conclude
that these people couldn't possibly be motivated. You'd be off
the mark if you did.

The truth is many of these individuals are very motivated. The
motivation they have though is usually poorly directed. They
may focus their energy toward something that you know is not
desirable or is a complete waste of time. Why would they do
this? They may not be able to tell you because their truth is often
masked – even from themselves.

Here's a rule to remember: *People do exactly what they want to do – even if they tell you otherwise.* If they truly don't want to do something, they will fight against it passively or actively not to do it – with as much energy to resist as required. Anyone trying to convince you differently is selling you a bogus bill of goods.

This is what I gleaned from the question out on the table: *This student was doing exactly what she was motivated to do.* In other words, her question showed that she was motivated to **not** accomplish the things she believed she should do in her life. I knew this and she was inviting me to give her advice.

In the past, I've refrained from giving such advice, and this time was no different. I started going in another direction by asking her some very blunt questions designed to put some good old-fashioned reality into the mix.

I asked the following:

1. What was your income last year?
2. What do you think it will be this year?
3. What could your income be this year, if you were doing exactly what you wanted to do, have nothing holding you back and always following through?
4. What is the difference between your answers to questions #1 and #3?

The class went through this little exercise with me and found the results eye opening. One person found a $63,000 difference. The others varied around that figure. They all got the main point: they were all performing far below their potential.

Then I dropped the bombshell. I told them that they were giving this amount of money away this year and probably had given it away in previous years, as well. I also told them that money was *not* the issue in their lack of performance. If money were the issue, they would not be giving it away.

Finally, I let the person who asked the question about motivational books know an important fact, the fact I said she already knew before she asked the question: *Motivation comes from within, not from without.* If a person is not motivated from within himself or herself, follow-through is haphazard at best. This is why people who enjoy what they do are the most motivated. Their energy is focused toward what they truly enjoy most. When that occurs, it's hard to hold them back. *They naturally provoke themselves toward unstoppable action!*

Bonus Connection – A dear friend shared with me the following: This concept hearkens back to your caveat at the beginning of this book. This book will not be of any help to you unless you *do something with it.* It's also why you express hope for this book to be bodacious. *If we enjoy it, we are more likely to make it our own and then our motivation will flow effortlessly.*

I agreed with him!

Provoking Success! (Coach's Review, Recommendations, Questions and Unreasonable Requests)

1. Determine what your nonperformance has cost you.
2. **Action Item:** Ask yourself if you're willing to continue paying this price any more.
3. Visualize YOUR dream. Find a provoking reason to excel.
4. **Action Item:** Create a plan and commit to it.
5. **Action Item:** Follow the dream you were truly intended to have. Let it flow. You deserve exactly what you create for yourself.

   Clarity is wonderfully motivating. – Coach John S. Nagy

30. Missing Something?

What one thing do you give to others that must also be kept by you to have any worth whatsoever? – Coach John S. Nagy

It happened again last week. I hadn't signed up for it and I would have been hugely irritated had I not already encountered it frequently enough in the past to be well prepared for it when it happened again. At 8:30 that morning, I extended a courtesy call to a client whom I was to meet an hour later. The call was received well and my client confirmed to me that he would be at our appointment and on time. With that confidence, I drove to our appointed destination. Arriving with some time to spare, I looked around the place for my client and concluded he had not yet arrived. I requested a table and reviewed my appointment file again in preparation for our visit.

I was not too concerned about filling in a few minutes with catch-up activities. I knew from my notes in his file that this client's coaching sessions starting an average of ten minutes late. I had come to expect tardiness from him and I had planned my appointment times accordingly. At the time, I held the belief that some patterns of behavior could be re-assuring. His file referenced a recently missed appointment, a missed call, and several late appointment starts – all with his apologies, of course.

I waited for quite a spell before deciding to give my client a call. Although being late was usual for him, the hour was slipping dangerously close to my departure time, if I were to be respectful to being on time for my next appointment.

When I called him, my client greeted me with surprise, as if I had jarred him back into this time zone. He let me know that right after receiving my confirmation call he had gotten a group of e-mails that required his immediate attention. Apologizing, he said he was only five minutes away and would be right over.

I noted the time. He arrived twelve minutes later. It was now thirty minutes past the appointment time. I figured it was time to talk about time management issues.

I thanked him for coming over. He apologized again for being late and changed the subject. I wasn't buying it. I chose to do my job as the coaching professional he was paying me to be. I asked him if he realized the impact of his actions. Looking startled that I would approach the topic again, he asked me what I meant.

I told him that the cost of non-performance was not immediately obvious to him. All he saw was that he was late. He didn't see how his actions over the last few weeks concerning his commitments to me had cost him, had cost me and had cost my other clients. I asked if he were open to hearing the gory details. He said yes.

I shared with him that the appointment last week that he had missed had cost me travel time and expenses that could have been avoided had I been notified in a timely fashion – With such notice, I could have made different arrangements with my time, resources and other client commitments. The client I had been with prior to his appointment might have used that time for further coaching. The client meeting with me after his appointment might have appreciated moving up her appointment time so she could get to other things sooner. The time I had set aside for the scheduled phone call from him that never occurred could have been used to take a walk with my family rather than staying in the office waiting for him to call.

The time he had missed in this coaching session was no different. I long ago learned to overlap my activities with fill work even though I'd much prefer to be in service to my clients rather than busying myself waiting for them to show up. Adding to the extra workload were the unnecessary phone calls I had to make to assure that my clients were okay, that there was nothing occurring in their lives to prevent them from following through on their commitments.

I stopped for a moment. I could see that my client was showing serious signs of discomfort. I could identify it from my own experiences with being coached. I let my client know that I hated being on the receiving end of this kind of information and knew what it was like. "My coach doesn't pull any punches, either" I told him, "and when I need feedback, he gives it, unsolicited. Although it's unsettling at times, I need to hear it because the behavior pattern he is telling me about is very likely manifesting itself in other areas of my life, as well.

My client spoke up. Yes, he found my words unsettling and yes, he still appreciated it. He had been seeing this pattern in many areas of his life and my bringing up the subject re-enforced to him the need for him to re-assess his priorities in all areas of his life. He smiled and thanked me.

Being "forward looking" in my approach, I asked him what he could do differently in the future. He said he would be contacting all others in advance who would be affected to let them know when his schedule changed. In the meanwhile, missed sessions with me could be handled by sending an immediate email or making a phone call once he knew that his schedule had changed. Missed phone calls could be avoided altogether by not making the commitment in the first place whenever he's on the road. Late arrivals could be dealt with more appropriately next time by contacting, via cell phone, the people who were to meet with him to let them know of his delay. He looked empowered as he spoke of his new approach.

We finished the coaching session on a high note. I asked him when he wanted to meet next and he quickly said, with a knowing smile, that he was unwilling to make a commitment right now. We both let out a hearty laugh.

We agreed that it would be okay to send emails back and forth over the next week until his schedule firmed up. Agreeing to this next phase, we both left for our next appointments.

I drove to my next appointment and arrived right on time. I called my next client after waiting just five minutes. He seemed startled that I was calling. He had forgotten our appointment due to other activities. I told him I would call him later to reschedule and I filled in the next hour with some activities that were scheduled for later that day. Talk about starting the day off right!

Here's a question for you: *Has this story provoked from you an answer to the question that I asked at the beginning of this chapter?*

Provoking Success! (Coach's Review, Recommendations, Questions and Unreasonable Requests)

1. When you ask another person to take action for your benefit, you are responsible for respecting his or her investment in you.

2. When something comes up which prevents you from following through on your commitments, you're responsible for notifying all parties affected in a timely fashion. Time is one resource you do not want to have people invest in with poor returns. A disrespect for time damages professional and personal relationships.

3. Excuse yourself enough and people will come to expect that your words cannot be trusted and that excuses are the only action they can count on from you.

4. Notification in a timely fashion means giving enough lead-time to reduce the impact on people who were extending themselves for you. Your non-performance in this matter will always affect more than just the person waiting.

5. Understand that there is a cost for non-performance beyond the immediate. Don't expect people to extend themselves for you once you've established a pattern of discourtesy toward their resources.

6. **Action Item:** *Provoke yourself toward considerate behavior for all involved.*

Your word is worthless if you don't keep it when given to others.
– Coach John S. Nagy

31. Trimming

Some folks harbor dead plants for years.
— Coach John S. Nagy

I've been working out in my garden these last few weeks. As I do every year, I assess those things that have benefit to the overall look and feel of the yard. Years ago, I learned something that improved my ability to assess such things. The lesson occurred one day when I noticed a hanging plant that a fellow worker had brought into his office.

I noticed immediately that the plant had big, shiny green leaves. What especially caught my attention was its appearance of overall health. I had the very same type of plant in my home, but it didn't have the same greenness or fullness that this co-worker's plant had. It got me thinking about why that was so.

I cared for my plant at home the best way I knew how. I was forever taking the new vine growth and looping it around its pot, yet it was sad-looking and sparse compared with the one at the office. I got riled thinking about the overall condition of my plant at home. The original purpose for having it was to have beauty that I could nurture and appreciate. It was no longer serving that purpose. I was in the presence of a "weed" that took more than it gave.

The next time I was around it I took a clipper to it and cut off about thirty feet of vine growth. I cropped a huge amount of overgrown root and dumped some new soil into the pot. The plant looked even more pitiful then before. Nevertheless, I thought maybe the loss of that entire excess vine might give the thing a better chance to grow. Wow, was I in for a delightful surprise.

During the next six weeks, I saw new growth burst out. The leaves were bright, shiny and huge. Within a very short time, the plant looked amazingly different from before the trimming. In disbelief, I shook my head and halfway expected it to rattle. Over the years, I had taken care of the plant; I had managed to water and feed it regularly. I even wrapped the new growth around the plant thinking I was somehow keeping all the hard work I put into it from going to waste. I didn't realize that this kind of thinking was holding back the health of the plant.

After my last-ditch effort to try something different, I realized what I should have been doing all the time. The plant *needed* me to crop it continuously as it grew in order to keep it in good health. The trimming made the root system work more effectively. Because I'd cut back the vine, it no longer drained away resources that the producing leaves needed to supply energy to the plant. It was beautiful!

That plant has now been twenty years in my care. It's as healthy as ever and has many offspring. Some are here at the old homestead and some are with friends who know how to give them good care. This brings me back to the present and doing my yard work.

I've used the same idea with the other plants around my yard. Trimming and cropping are now a natural part of the goings-on around here. The shrubs and trees get this too. No longer do I just water and fertilize. Grooming is now done regularly. I no longer give effort to things that are not contributing to the overall health of my plants.

Come to think about it, I operate the same way in business and in life. There are times when trimming is the appropriate thing to do when clients, personnel, and even friends who are no longer contributing to the overall health of my business or life. Sure, they're physically present. They're just are not contributing in the positive manner they once did.

I've learned too, that trimming must be done in an honoring way. Sometimes it's done as periodic "housecleaning" that is best for all involved. At other times, it has become clear that the people I serve are at a point where I can best serve them by referring them to other professional services. In either case, the process of transition should be as honorable as the process of providing service – respecting those who are involved at all times.

Trimming should never be confused with doing a hatchet job. Hatchet jobs always leave someone bleeding. Trimming is always a win/win for everyone involved, especially when you have "honoring" in mind during the process. Some actions you can take to do this are:

1. Acknowledge to yourself and the other party that things have changed.
2. Discuss the ramifications of the change on the relationship.
3. Ask yourself and the others involved if a shift to a new purpose is appropriate or perhaps desired.
4. If so, then start the process of creating that purpose. If not, then celebrate the conclusion, support each other in the transition and get closure.

There's a saying that some people don't often hear: *Every relationship serves a purpose and, once served, it will change to serve a new purpose even if the relationship no longer supports the original intent.* Because relationships transform like this, they can change into something detrimental for the people involved. That's why it's always a good idea to keep in mind the purpose of a relationship. Do this consciously! There are client relationships that come to term. There are friendships, struck from common interests, which fade as common interests fade. There are relationships, carved from common experiences, which no longer hold the spotlight for either party. No matter what the case may be, recognizing what provoked and held the relationship together allows for an honoring transition should a turning point occur. Letting go then becomes part of a relationship's growth.

To respect any relationship, business, personal, or otherwise, means to honor it. This means when the relationship is of service to you and after its purposes have been served.

Coach's Note: *Here's a provoking question for you. When's the last time you did some well-needed trimming?*

Provoking Success! (Coach's Review, Recommendations, Questions and Unreasonable Requests)

1. **Action Item:** Provoke yourself toward examining your business and life to identify things that are "overgrown or dead."

2. **Action Item:** Check all parts for contribution toward your purpose.

3. **Action Item:** Remove those parts that no longer contribute to the overall purpose.

4. **Action Item:** Either find a new purpose for that which was trimmed or allow it to find a new one for itself.

5. **Action Item:** Honor that which has been removed; Nurture that which remains.

Trimming is conscious "letting go" and a good habit for a healthy life. – Coach John S. Nagy

32. A Simple & Honest (Business) Plan

A good plan is essential in both business and life.
– Coach John S. Nagy

Many small and mid-size companies find that creating or updating their business plan is one of their biggest challenges. To be effective, a plan must be honest and direct enough to enable the owner and staff to move right along with the growth of their business. Whether your company is a startup or one that's been in operation for some time, having a document that clearly explains your business "instruction set" and "vision" will benefit your business tremendously.

Many businesses use a simple Question and Answer (Q&A) format to get this often-daunting task underway. This approach addresses most, if not all, of the basic issues a small to mid-size business needs to cover during a normal business planning or evaluation stage.

Keep in mind that business plans are meant to be "living" documents. They should serve as a guide to direct your business wherever you want it to go. Please don't ever look at the business plan that is being shared here as a concrete instruction set; rather, please look at it as a set of clear-cut supporting guidelines to help you bring about what you want.

This "Business Plan" when…

- Honest - causes little or no friction with your business choices, long after the plan has been committed to paper. (Dishonest plans, conscious or not, always cause problems long term because your covert intent won't support your overt actions.)
- Proper - will restore clarity wherever focus has faded.

142

- Reviewed rigorously - keeps you on track and prevents you from straying from your original intent.

- Applied - affords you measurements that reveal your company's progress.

- Used openly - engenders trust in you from people who want to do business with you. They will trust your services and products long into the future.

- Used purposefully - aligns your resources & people into a synergistic, unstoppable force.

Ironically, the very chapter you're reading now is itself a plan that was written to assist you in writing such a plan for yourself. It should help you to keep your plan simple, uncomplicated and, above all, meaningful. You need to meet these criteria in order to produce the supportive document you desire.

It's a good idea to avoid using the business plan we are creating here as a selling tool to banks and investment institutions. Formal business plans for these groups are different from what we're looking at here. Your document should involve everything you need to bring about success in your business, and should be a useful guide for meeting your intended aim. Whether or not it later serves to help you acquire financial support for your venture is superfluous to the immediate intent. Be sure to *put it in writing*. Writing clarifies your end-in-mind. If you write down your plan clearly enough for another person to read and fully understand, then you own it; if you can't do this, then it owns you. This is because an unclear plan will deliver unclear results. The process of writing down a plan clearly, clear enough for another person to comprehend what you intend to do, usually means that you are clear on it yourself. If you can't do this, then you are putting your intentions at risk of failure. Lack of clarity brings uncertainty of actions and outcomes. As a result, you become "owned" by that fuzziness because it has more control over the outcome than you do. You want a document that supports your total ownership and delivery of what you wish to achieve. With clarity comes ownership.

What are the questions you want to ask? First, look at the areas to consider:

1. Inside-Out View – Your Being and Your Doing
2. Outside-In View – Your Target
3. Connections Between the Two – Getting Their Attention
4. Budget – Your Expense Flow
5. Profit – Your ROI (Return on Investment)
6. Future – Your five-year projection
7. Executive Summary – Your Overview

Each of these seven areas covers a different aspect of the plan. If you're interested, at the end of this book is a chapter containing questions you can ask yourself about each of these sections. Please take the time to answer the questions in detail, because the clearer your plan is, the more likely its viability will be.

Once you've put your responses to these questions on paper, you should get a reality check on your writing. Identify business people whom you trust to help you review your plan for any gaps and/or inconsistencies. Empower each of these people to feel free to be honest with their thoughts and suggestions. Prepare yourself ahead of time to be amazed by what you'll hear and by how grateful you'll be for their provoking you toward greater success.

Provoking Success! (Coach's Review, Recommendations, Questions and Unreasonable Requests)

1. **Action Item:** Create your business plan as honestly as you can. If you're new to this, do the best you can and ask for help. If you don't know something, do the best you can and ask for help. If similarly operated successful businesses usually take at least six months to show a profit, don't set yourself a timeline of three months – it's both unrealistic and dishonest.

2. **Action Item:** Cover everything that you need to guide you along the path of success. Profit and loss estimates are a basic to business. What would adding procedural manuals, conflict resolution procedures and interaction policies do for you?

3. **Action Item:** Get honest opinions from knowledgeable professionals on your effort. A mentor, Coach, CPA, bookkeeper, attorney, peer and even SBA (Small Business Administration) personnel can all offer insights into things you will miss because you're too close to what you're planning to see the entire picture.

4. **Action Item:** Be open to review and revise as you create and use your plan. Adjustments don't mean that you got it wrong; they mean that you're able to improve what you are creating.

5. Be aware that even if you're operating a department within an organization, – a specific business plan still applies. It's just plan good business sense to have a plan to work and to work a plan.

Businesses grow, as should the plans that assist in that growth.

Uncommon Contracts, Negotiations, and Agreements

Be absolutely and unequivocally clear regarding any agreements you make. – Coach John S. Nagy

33. Who's the Customer?

It's surprising how many people think that the person with the cash is the only customer. – *Coach John S. Nagy*

I hope that reading this chapter will shake up your reality – in a "good way" of course. It came to be written as the result of a thought provoking conversation I had with a client. Our conversation revealed a specific mindset held by many in the business world and the public at-large. That mindset relates to a unilateral view of who the customer actually is.

To illustrate this mindset at work, let's look at a situation. Suppose you go to purchase a vehicle at your local car dealership, discuss with the salesperson the purchase of a vehicle, the salesperson shows a number of vehicles to you, you find one that meets your needs, sign the papers on the deal, and put down cash to seal the transaction. You drive your new car off the lot feeling satisfied that you made a good deal. The people involved in this situation are you and the dealership, represented by the salesperson.

Ponder the following. The question is, "Who is really the customer here?" Please take a little time to think about this. You've probably already realized that the obvious answer is not the answer we're looking for.

If you have the typical response of most people, your response is that the customer is obviously you. What most people with this particular mindset fail to realize is that, although you *are* the one purchasing the car with your money, the salesperson is also purchasing your money with his car.

Another way to state this is to say that one person in the deal purchases products or services with cash equivalents and the other person in the deal purchases cash equivalents with products or services.

It doesn't matter whether the person is purchasing with cash equivalents, products or services. Anyone purchasing anything is a customer.

Are we going into brain overload yet?

If you try to do business while still holding on to this unilateral mindset, you will fail to realize the benefits of seeing that the person you are dealing with is as much a customer to you as you are to them. Remember, all deals can be equitable (win-win) if worked right. You have to provide to the person you're dealing with enough "value" for them to want to exchange what they have for what you have.

Thinking in a "win-win" manner has been shared in many ways for a long time. It is often associated with Stephen Covey who conveyed this concept in his "Seven Habits of Highly Effective People" book. As I understand it, for one person to engage in activity with another such that both benefit, both parties must be obtaining something of greater value from the engagement. Understanding and practicing this concept is what can begin to make your business deals "win-win" situations.

The next time you find yourself purchasing from an individual or a group, place yourself into the mind-set that they are *your* customers too even though you might be the one providing the cash element of the deal. When you do, ask yourself the following question, "Is what I'm offering to the other party equitable enough for them to want to be my customer?" Should your answer be "no," provoke yourself toward further action. What might that action be? How about reassessing the deal and working toward something that is more equitable?

In addition, if you consider that within any business having multiple parties involved, all those people within that business could be considered internal customers. Internal customers could include your boss, your coworkers, subordinates, etc. You could also include people in other departments. People outside the company could be considered external customers.

Coach's Note: *It doesn't end here though. Did you know that people you deal with in your social and family circles are also your customers? Does this provoke you toward something more to consider? I hope so!*

Provoking Success! (Coach's Review, Recommendations, Questions and Unreasonable Requests)

1. When you transcend the cash element of any agreement you see that everybody involved in the deal is a customer.
2. **Action Item:** Identify the situations you have **not** thought of yourself as being a customer while you were purchasing money with your services or product.
3. How might you provide better service to your customers, even if you are the one selling your cash in exchange for what the other customer is offering? **Action Item:** Write this out.
4. How might you provide better service to your customers, even if you are dealing with people who don't consider you their customer? **Action Item:** Write this out.
5. How might this new way of looking at who a customer really is be of help to you in your business? Can you apply this idea in other parts of your life? **Action Item:** Write this out.

When you view and treat everyone as a customer, you position yourself much more favorably to maximize all agreements.
– Coach John S. Nagy

34. Learning the "Nutshell" Benefit

Briefitize! – Coach John S. Nagy

Most of us have heard the acronym, KISS for "Keep It Successfully Simple." There is much benefit when we learn to *keep it brief.* Learn to "nutshell" your communications. You'll benefit all involved. That should be enough and I could end there. Yet, if I didn't say more, many of you might not know the full ramifications of what I mean. So I'll risk being verbose and perhaps ruin the point by explaining.

Keep it brief. I'll be blunt. If you're a talker and like to have people listen to you more than you like to listen to them (doing this is called "taking captives"), you may want to pay attention. Nothing is more frustrating then waiting patiently for your turn to talk and it never comes. If you're finding that people interrupt you continuously, instead of simply thinking of them as being rude, you might want to consider that they may be letting you take a breather so you can continue after their turn to speak. After all, if you go on, you'll either "pass out" from lack of oxygen or be "passed on" by people trying to avoid you." Your captive isn't being rude; he or she is practicing self-preservation in the midst of an assault! (You know – Overwhelm!)

Keep it brief. The bonds you wish to create with others through your conversations require active participants, not passive listeners. People do not want to be held hostage, waiting for you to finish saying all that you believe they need to hear. Many people will patiently wait for their turn, silently suffering and hoping to persevere while their captor rambles on. Monopolizing the conversation with excessive details doesn't give the other party a chance to ask for any necessary clarifying questions or reflect back that they understand what you've said. The acronym TMI means "Too much information." Too much is always just that: too much. Information overloads turn off listening.

Moreover, if nobody were listening to you, why would you want to continue talking? Respect your audience. If you want an equal, treat your listener as an equal.

Keep it brief. Answer the question and only the question. Metaphors apply here: Too much water with too little drainage causes roots to rot; too much to eat with too little digestion prevents nourishment. Conversations are similar. A little at a time is much easier to stomach. Unnecessary expounding or un-requested detailing burdens listeners with more than they wanted to know. Respond in kind and give the other party equal time. Engage them in your sharing. Show them that you're interested in what your conversation partner has to say. Even conversations between a professional and a client require consideration. Give it and you'll receive consideration in return.

Keep it brief. Your clients, co-workers, boss and "significant others" will all appreciate it. Others value your respect for them above all else. It's a good investment, with high returns for all involved.

Keep it brief. The greatest leaders listen more than they talk. The greatest communicators are also the greatest listeners. Our anatomy* backs this up. Take it in. Think about it!

Keep it brief. The time you save is truly your own.

Provoke brevity!

Nutshell.**

Benefits? You bet!

Provoking Success! (Coach's Review, Recommendations, Questions and Unreasonable Requests)

1. **Action Item:** Contribute to conversation to keep it going, not to dominate it.
2. **Action Item:** Add just enough to contribute and no more.
3. **Action Item:** NUTSHELL!
4. If you aren't sure when to stop talking just ask someone. You're probably overdue to stop.
5. Pay attention to how you feel when someone has proven himself or herself to be better at capturing you and holding you hostage than you were. Which is getting more attention, their words or your growing resentment and frustration? Don't put anyone else in the position of feeling that way towards you!
6. The best way to know if people want you to talk more is if they ask you a question.
7. If you don't strike oil, quit boring!
8. **Action Item:** After having read this chapter, go back to the questions at the end of the "Who's the Customer" chapter and answer them with the idea in mind that you and your partner are each other's customers with conversation as the product being sold.
9. **Action Item:** TMI put forth? Briefitize!

* We have two ears and just one mouth. This gives us a two to one ratio for listening to speaking.

** Make it compact enough to fit inside the shell of a nut.

Be succinct! – Coach John S. Nagy

35. One Man's Secret

What would it take to ruin your meal? – Coach John S. Nagy

I was reminded one evening of a story I'd heard years ago. I was speaking with a client about a job situation and it became evident that he felt some strong reservations regarding the feasibility of the opportunity. It was during that conversation that I remembered and shared this tale with him.

In truth, I have no idea as to the source or validity of the story. I've found it to be an anchor of wisdom for me and I hoped that it would be for my client, as well. Aspects of his situation reflected to me the many times I had needed to make a decision about whether or not to hire a client. When push comes to shove, this story provokes me toward keeping things in perspective.

Let me share it with you now:

An inquisitive business novice asked an old-timer as to what he attributed his unparalleled success. The old-timer didn't hesitate in his response. He said that the reason he was so successful was because he learned to treat business opportunities as if they were meals.

The first thing he had learned was to approach deals only if they smelled right. He invested great faith in his nose to be his front line assessment tool. If the opportunity didn't smell right, he cleared out of the area. He had come to understand that if the odor was bad, he didn't even want the possibility of having his clothes absorb the fumes! He knew that if that were to happen, others would smell where he had been and that was not good for his business.

The old-timer continued with his response by saying that if a deal smelled right he would then take just a bit of the deal into his mouth to get a sense of what its flavor was. If it didn't taste right, he would spit it out and pass on the opportunity. Anything that had an unpleasant taste for him would be just as unpleasant for any others with whom he would be dealing. He couldn't see asking others to savor something he himself didn't like.

If it tasted right, then he swallowed it to see if it swallowed or went down easily. If it didn't, he would bow out on the rest of the offering. It didn't bother him to do this even if he'd already paid for the meal (deal) in full. He figured that the personal cost to his stomach for filling it with something that didn't go down easily was far greater than the cost of the deal. He found that forgiving himself and cutting his losses was easier on his gut than putting something in it that he felt was wrong.

If the deal did swallow easily, he would then allow it to sit in his gut for a while. If it didn't settle right or if it caused an unpleasant aftereffect he would never give the "cook" another chance. He figured that anyone professing to be a "cook," whose offerings caused upset stomachs, should be avoided.

The old-timer added there had been a few times when what at first seemed to fail his criteria for acceptance really was acceptable. When that occurred, it was usually because he wasn't feeling "quite together" to begin with. He smiled and winked at the upstart as he said, "But that's another story."

Provoking Success! (Coach's Review, Recommendations, Questions and Unreasonable Requests)

1. Treat every opportunity as if it were a meal.

2. **Action Item:** Take a whiff and assess its odor. Proceed only if it smells pleasant.

3. **Action Item:** Taste it and assess its flavor. Continue only if found savor-worthy.

4. **Action Item:** Swallow a bit of it and assess how it sits. Carry on only if it's comforting and feels good to you.

5. **Action Item:** Assess the results. Ask yourself if you would care to give the "cook" another chance.

6. **Action Item:** Provoke yourself toward partaking in those meals that you know will sit well and nurture your needs.

Successful people have good taste and they trust their gut.
– Coach John S. Nagy

36. I See, I See

When negotiations seem difficult, if you break the process down into its respective elements, your path will become clearer and simpler and so will your choices. – Coach John S. Nagy

Years ago, while mediating a difficult negotiation, I came up with a simple and effective acronym that's helped me successfully resolve situations and do it with little or no conflict. I base this simple acronym on an even simpler premise: "shared perceptions help create harmony." Perceptions shape our reality and we make decisions and choices based on the reality we perceive. When we shift our perceptions, or look at something in a different way, we shift our reality; therefore, the choices we make can change dramatically. Many conflicts can be avoided if all of the involved parties can acknowledge that the *perceptions* of the others have some validity. A willingness to do this can do a lot to build bridges across seemingly impassable chasms.

Some people believe that acknowledging the other party's position is the same as giving in, that being the least bit open to seeing the other person's point of view weakens their own position. While this belief is understandable, the truth lies miles away: Most people argue their *positions* rather than their *interests*. The distinction between the two is as simple as understanding that people have chosen to "take a specific stand" on an issue rather than focus on getting their interests served. For example, I may say that I'm not going to do a certain task because it was someone else's responsibility to do (I take a *position* on a specific action) even though doing the task will get my needs met (Doing the task serves my *interests*.) While opening yourself to hear the other side may well weaken your *position*, it also gives a greater opportunity to serve the *interests* of both parties, which makes for a much better resolution.

Please understand that acknowledgment does **not** mean you are in agreement with the other party. Acknowledgment merely lets the other side know that, in spite of your differences, you're aware of how they perceive the situation (and may even possibly understand it.) It should never infer anything else. All acknowledgment does is let the other side know that you're willing to be open to seeing the situation differently than you are now seeing it.

That's the wonder of the acronym I use. It shifts the perception of those who use it without causing them to lose sight of their own interests. It helps people move toward resolution by getting the *interests,* instead of the *positions,* of both parties out on the table. Once the interests are out in plain view, both parties can then gain clarity on how they need to proceed in order to put the issues to rest.

The acronym for the concepts I'm sharing here is "ICIC" and it's a play on the words and forms the phrase "I see I see." You can use it as a reminder to help in two ways. First, just saying it lets the other party know that we "get it" and we understand what's being shared. Second, it reminds us to stay open to the perceptions of the other party so we can continue to "get it." The same goes for the other party's "getting it," too.

The first letter in our acronym (ICIC) is "I" and stands for "**issues**." Issues are the problems, challenges and opportunities each party has which surround a specific situation. Positions are usually taken on issues. Both parties need to have clarity on what issues need to be addressed and in what order of priority. By putting all the issues on the table, each party has the opportunity to express their side of things and listen to the other party's view. Sometimes people are fuzzy, or unclear, on the issues and by putting the issues "out on the table," both parties can get a "reality check" which can help them focus on what brought them to the negotiating table in the first place.

The second letter is "C" for "**concerns**." Once the issues are clearly perceived by both parties, the potential ramifications of each issue for each party need to be stated as concerns. The act of stating one's concerns has tremendous power, as it helps greatly to clarify the motivations and the priorities of each of the involved parties. It also opens up opportunities for both sides to continue building bridges toward resolution. I have often participated in mediations where a concern was stated by one party, then addressed, and quickly put to rest by the other party in a manner satisfactory to the interests of both parties. If the concern had not been stated and then addressed satisfactorily, it would have greatly hampered the progress of the mediation.

The third letter is "I" for "**interests**." Once each party has stated their issues and concerns, the next step is to address each party's interests. As implied earlier, "interests" are what each party would like to receive from the negotiations. Expression of interests helps each party work together toward ways for each party to be served. Most of the time, both parties can do this with mutual satisfaction. The typical example of this is the "all or nothing" scenario involving an orange. Both parties want the orange (each party takes a position in the belief that their interest will be served). One wants it for the peel. The other wants it for the juice. We see each party's own true interests but they are unknown to the other party, which is why they are in negotiations.

Please remember that any "negotiation" is made much more difficult when the involved parties are not clear about *all* the interests that need be served. Focusing on the interests of all parties helps clear up the fuzziness and allows another bridge to be built.

The fourth and last letter is "C" for "**considerations**." Once everything else has been put on the table for each party to view and gain clarity, the parties then need to "express their considerations." It's a pleasant way to say what concessions each party is willing to give for the purpose of resolution. Very often, when we're trying to negotiate with someone and one of us expresses what we are willing to do in order to resolve any remaining conflict, the other party will "follow suit." It's important to do this only *after* everything else has been put on the table. Carrying out this step before you reach this stage may weaken the ability of the other party to see your point of view.

To use the "ICIC" acronym effectively, both parties must have enough time to express their issues, concerns, interests, and then their considerations without interruption. During the course of the negotiations, it is very helpful to pause and reflect or mirror back to each other during each stage along the way. Each party should be able to reflect back what the other has been saying to that person's satisfaction.

In other words, I listen to your issues and share what I understand about them back to you as clearly as I can. Once you are satisfied that I understand, then you do the same for me. We then go to the next stage and repeat the process through to the end.

I've used this tool many times since I first created it. It's become a natural part of my mediating and negotiating styles. Like other people, I strive for win-win conditions. It's just good business.

Coach's Note: *This tool isn't limited to potential business conflicts. It works in virtually any professional and personal circumstances. Life can often be a series of negotiations. Tools that help us navigate successfully with others in mind benefit everyone. If appropriate, why not use a simple tool to cause outcomes that are the best possible? Provoke yourself toward using tools for greater success.*

Provoking Success! (Coach's Review, Recommendations, Questions and Unreasonable Requests)

In any kind of negotiations:

1. **Action Item:** Be clear on what your **issues** are and give equal opportunity for the issues of the other side to be heard and acknowledged by you.

2. **Action Item:** Be clear as to what your **concerns** are and give equal opportunity for the concerns of the other side to be heard and acknowledged by you.

3. **Action Item:** Be clear as to what your **interests** are and give equal opportunity for the interests of the other side to be heard and acknowledged by you.

4. **Action Item:** Be clear as to what your **considerations** are and give equal opportunity for the considerations of the side to be heard and acknowledged by you.

5. Learn to say, "I see I see!" and you will discover more than you imagined possible.

6. **Action Item:** Provoke yourself toward ways to use this technique when you encounter situations involving teams, family, friends, co-workers and business connections where clarity would help the progress of any common effort.

Negotiations start with a willingness to listen.
– Coach John S. Nagy

37. Wooden Shoes

*If you're not getting forward motion, check to see
what's clogging your gears. – Coach John S. Nagy*

It just wasn't happening. No matter what my client tried to do to overcome the obstacle, the results were still the same – success was beyond her reach.

It took some intense analysis of the situation before we were able to figure out what was preventing her wheels from moving forward. In the end, the root cause of it was finally uncovered and my client was able to move on.

What was the root cause? What could possibly have prevented the success she so sorely desired?

I could go into a great story here and point my finger at all the easily seen details that compose the surface of the problem. I could present all the connections between those surface details and the root cause of the problem that made it have such a negative impact on her desired outcome. If I were to do that, the whole point of this story would be lost. What I will offer instead is a spotlight on a stark reality that permeates almost all stories where desired progress doesn't occur – no matter what the effort.

That root cause is "sabotage." Not the kind of sabotage you see in the movies where an enemy spy or collaborator is planting a device, cutting a brake line, or sawing part way through a support beam. It is simple everyday sabotage. It's brought about by distraction, inattention to details, non-follow through, and a basket full of other "excuses" we tend to offer as reasons for things not moving forward.

You might be saying "**Me**! Sabotage **my** efforts? **Never!**" and you might actually be right in your thinking. If you are facing a situation where "things are not moving forward" well for you, then you might actually be wrong – especially if you haven't considered how you may be contributing to the situation you're in.

Before you say "huh?" to this, let me take a side path first and then come back to my assertion. Let's examine the origins of the word "sabotage" briefly and then see how it might apply to your situation.

The word "sabotage" originated in northern Europe as a description for, and an honoring of, an event that occurred many years ago. It seems that some factory workers at the time didn't like how the management was running the mill. As a sign of protest, they endeavored to throw their shoes into the turning gears of the mill.

Now this wouldn't have been so bad if the shoes had been made of leather or a similar soft material. Most mill gears of that time were strong and could have withstood even a few pieces of thick leather. Unfortunately, for the owner of the mill, the shoes were made not of leather but of wood. Because of the worker's actions, their wooden shoes jammed up the gears and all forward movement of the gears ceased.

In commemoration of that fateful event, the fine art of throwing wooden shoes (called "sabots") into the moving gears of a process thereby causing that process to cease working, has come to be known, as "sabotage."

Modern day usage of the word "sabotage" has come to denote any situation where desired activities aren't realized due to interference. That interference doesn't have to be conscious, overt, planned, deliberate or otherwise. It just has to occur for it to be sabotage.

This is what my client's situation was. The desired results weren't there and it was a direct result of sabotage – a variety of wooden shoes stuck in her gears. To create a positive change, she had to identify each wooden shoe that interfered with her success and remove it. It this way, the progress she truly desired could occur. Once she had done this, my client saw a marked improvement in her ability to obtain the results she desired. She also took this insight about sabotage and found she could apply it in many other areas of her life with similar outcomes.

Admittedly, at first it was not a comfortable process for her. It demanded that she examine her procedures for obtaining her desired outcomes. Going through this process reflected back to her the contributions she herself had been making to how things "did and didn't" get done. It required her to take ownership of her own work and personal habits that had been contributing to her self-sabotage so she could begin making changes in her own behaviors.

Of course, the results of these efforts benefited her immensely. She forged some new behaviors that gave her quicker results. The efforts she was now able to make required less investment from her because she was no longer working against herself She felt less stress and less drain. She had more energy and her smile started to appear more often.

This all occurred because she chose to get rid of the wooden shoes, the sabots, in her life.

Coach's Note: This would only be a good story if it provoked a benefit for you. Let's get back on track and do just that – make all of this personal. *Have you checked lately to see how many wooden shoes you've got clogging up your life?* No? When *are* you going to open the lid on your stopped processes and look at some serious shoe removal?

Provoking Success! (Coach's Review, Recommendations, Questions and Unreasonable Requests)

1. Sabotages are any things that prevent progress from occurring.
2. Sabotage can come in many forms and they fall into both action and non-action categories.
3. **Action Item:** Challenge yourself to identify at least 10 sabotages in your life.
4. **Action Item:** Enlist the aid of others who are close to you to help you identify even more.
5. **Action Item:** Create an action plan to implement for all the sabotages you've identified. Have others help you if they can.
6. **Action Item:** Implement your plan when you realize sabotage is occurring,

Keep yourself, not your shoes, in gear. – Coach John S. Nagy

38. Getting to Agreement

Don't ask me to invest more of myself for your benefit than you're willing to invest of yourself. – Coach John S. Nagy

Recently a client brought to my attention a situation that is nearly universal to business owners providing a service to people. It's especially problematic to people, like my client, who were new to running a service business. He was in a state of agitation and showed all the signs of a man experiencing maximum frustration. He had once again found himself in a position where he realized he did not have a comprehensive and solid contract – only he didn't see this was the cause of his frustration.

He'd been asked by one of his clients to work on a particular problem until a solution was found. Because his client had seemed very concerned about the problem, he took the initiative. He stayed up all night working on it, and was able to come up with a viable solution. When he offered the solution to his client, after a night's labor, all he received was a "thanks" for his efforts. His client then put all the hard work on the shelf and took no action at all to implement the solution.

That's when my client's unsettled feelings began. Over the next few days, he grew progressively disturbed at his client's inaction. It was really eating at him. The effort he had expended on his client's behalf was not paying off. To make matter's worse, his client did not plan to take action on his work. My client sat before me with an obvious expression of utter exhaustion. Clearly, this was not the first time he had had this kind of experience. Wearier this time, more than ever before, he was open to some suggestions.

We explored what had caused this turn of events. We evaluated the way he went about obtaining the agreement for the job and the work that was to be done. During our discussion, we discovered a pattern of behavior that had allowed his current, as well as past, situations to occur:

His previous agreements had lacked three key components:

- The first was *clarity* about what both parties wanted and what both sides were promising to deliver.
- The second was *how his client would fairly compensate* him for each phase of effort.
- The third was a *clearly defined timeframe* for implementation of each phase of the work requested.

My client realized that he needed to create a process for making agreements that would assure all three of these components were in place.

To avoid misunderstandings with his clients, he needed to spell out in writing what specific actions he was committing himself to undertake on his client's behalf. He had to state clearly and specifically what was expected from his client in return. If his client was merely looking for a solution to consider (but not take prompt action upon), then that would be the scope of the job and compensation for that phase of his work would be expected. If the second phase of the job was for the solution to be implemented by my client, then compensation for the first phase work could be rolled into the second phase according to specific agreed upon terms. As specifically as possible: There should be a clear understanding about whether there would be a delay between the first and second phases of the job. There should be a clear understanding about what the terms for billing would be if the second phase were not to be implemented within the designated time.

This brings into focus a concept that business "old-timers" understand and implement without fail, because to do otherwise would result in failure. Although I tell my clients about this principle, many new business owners forget to put it into effect.

So what is this concept that many forget? It's called "equity of action." This means that "you should undertake only those actions that have been authorized" and "you should make sure beforehand that the authorized actions you plan to undertake on behalf of another have a guaranteed reciprocal outcome for both parties involved" – even if it's only "in part." Please let me explain what I mean by "in part": Components of an agreement, or contract, which bring about a win/win situation for both parties, are based on equity of action. If the end-goal of a contract is truly to have a problem solved, then finding the solution to the problem is only the first of two necessary actions that need to be authorized.

The second action necessary to have a problem solved is to implement the solution. If, as it was with my client's employer, he is not willing to authorize you to follow through on something he has asked you to do, then he has only authorized you "in part." Moreover, authorization, in full or in part, needs to include compensation in order to have "equity of action."

If a client is asking you to invest yourself for their benefit, you should expect them to do the same for you. If an action is requested, compensation for the action should follow. For equity to exist, your action of requested service must be in exchange for their action of giving requested compensation. If the client is unwilling to promise compensation for all phases of service that they want you to promise to complete, it's a good indication they want something for nothing. They're indicating the importance of their interaction with you; i.e., not much.

The solution to this situation is to have in place a process that provokes a win/win scenario for both parties. If your potential client agrees to this process, you'll have a win/win situation underway. If they do not agree to it, then you'll have invested little of your time or resources and still have a positive situation. Committing to this process will prevent many futile actions. The results will be more fruitful and fulfilling for all.

Provoking Success! (Coach's Review, Recommendations, Questions and Unreasonable Requests)

1. **Action Item:** Make sure any action another person requests you to make is backed up with the authority for you to carry it out.

2. **Action Item:** Make sure an agreement compensates you for any actions you take on their behalf.

3. **Action Item:** Determine a clear length of time for decisions, compensation and phases of the project.

4. **Action Item:** If the client is unwilling to invest, respond in kind.

5. **Action Item:** Get it in writing.

Discuss a fair equity arrangement upfront.
– Coach John S. Nagy

39. Very Curious Equity Ethics

When you expect more from others than you're willing to give of yourself, life sure gets rough. – Coach John S. Nagy

A client of mine and I were engaged in a conversation the other day and she brought up her feelings of hurt about the seemingly simple (at first) topic of her not being invited out to lunch. This "simple topic" gave us some fertile ground for growth by giving her some profound insights into her expectations of others.

I could understand her feelings of being upset. She enjoyed going out to lunch with others. Over the past year or so, she had become painfully aware that many people who used to invite her had stopped asking. We began our ensuing discussion by giving recognition to the enjoyment that she felt from sharing lunchtime companionship and the sadness that she felt when she saw others going out and leaving her behind.

I asked her how much she enjoyed going out to lunch. She said, "Lots." I asked her how she felt when others asked her to go. She said, "Great!" I asked her when she was last invited out to lunch. It had been so long that she couldn't remember. Then I asked her the big one, "When was the last time you asked someone out to lunch?"

Her mouth dropped open and her face turned red with embarrassment. She'd gotten the message: She had been showing, through her actions, that she had not been willing to extend to others what she wanted extended to her. "Wow!" was all she said. They did not invite her because she had not been inviting them.

She smiled and commented that she now knew what she had to do. I asked her to commit to inviting others out to lunch during the upcoming month and letting me know what happened. The next day I got a voice mail message from my client. She had started that day, during her morning break, to ask people out to lunch. The next thing she knew, she was getting inbound calls asking her when she would be available to go out. She was simply ecstatic. Then again, isn't that how integrity works?

It's interesting to see how simple integrity issues like this are worked out. The flipside of this is not as fun. I've heard business professionals in countless offices complain that they leave messages for someone and rarely get a response back, yet these same complainers are the first ones to erase a voice mail if they believe the call is not worth a response.

These people don't see a connection between their not responding to others and others not responding to them. The fact is we attract what we put out. Others are merely reflecting back the same attitude that was presented to them. Ironically enough, they (the complainers) expect from others what they themselves are often unwilling to give. They don't realize how much they contribute to this.

You may feel free to call me a throwback on this issue. It's a rare occurrence when I don't respond to voicemail or email queries, especially when the request is from someone who is looking specifically for me. Mind you, I ditch computer-generated spam and junk mail without a second thought. Nevertheless, when a businessperson takes the time to leave me a message, I call back. I, too, am in business and I know what it's like to be on the receiving end of a non-response so I don't want to add to the annoyance. I'm a firm believer that not returning well-intentioned calls increases the odds of that same action happening to me. To me, it's hypocritical to complain about something that I do myself.

As for the "inconsiderates" of the world – those people who do not return well-intentioned calls - their numbers are legion. Any message sent their way to help "set them straight" often falls on deaf ears. The sad reality is that they are where they need to be. The good news is that we don't have to sit there with them.

Once we accept this reality, inconsiderateness can actually be the basis for some great humor. A series of events I experienced can best illustrate this. It started with an e-mail that came my way. The message had a clear sense of urgency in its energy and wording:

> "I am looking to find a coach to begin work on myself immediately. I am looking to take my communications many levels up. Contact me directly at <Phone #1> during the day or <Phone #2> in the evenings or by e-mailing me back. I hope to hear from you soon as I would like to begin this week. Thanks, <Name> "

In his message, the person had asked me to respond quickly. His objective was clear: he wanted to take his "communications up many levels." This was an excellent goal and one that I knew I could help him. I took action immediately and responded by leaving messages at both of his phone numbers and by emailing him as well. This was, after all, all about communication!

Three weeks passed by. The person never responded. Being considerate, my mind started wondering in a considerate way. It was possible that my e-mail to him might not have gone through and the phone messages I left at his home and office might accidentally have been erased. Stranger things have happened in my own office and I didn't want to believe he would ask me to do something and not follow through in return. As always, I gave him the benefit of the doubt since I didn't know the whole story. After a few days more, I sent a second, follow-up, e-mail to provoke a possible update from him.

To his credit, I did eventually get an e-mail back – 30 days later. He said he was "working with a great coach" with "things going quite well." He thanked me for the professional follow-up I had done and even told me about the possibility of referring future business to me. He had not yet reached the point in his coaching to understand the message his behavior communicated to others.

As for me, if I had wanted to purchase a good second story about irony, I could not have bought better material for which to write. The guy definitely had the right objective in mind when he said he wanted to improve his communication skills and he was even able to appreciate this skill when he saw in others. Could he practice it himself? Could he recognize his discourtesies enough to correct them? I sure hope his coach provokes him toward a better understanding of what that skill involves.

Coach's Note: *After thinking about the irony of all this I couldn't help wondering if this last guy has been invited to lunch lately.*

Provoking Success! (Coach's Review, Recommendations, Questions and Unreasonable Requests)

1. Expect the same actions from yourself that you would want to see in others.

2. **Action Item:** Look at what you complain about in others as a possible reflection of what you can improve in your own actions & attitudes towards them. Create a list with actions that will improve your behavior in these matters.

3. Inconsiderate people are perfect examples to provoke your awareness and improve your integrity.

4. **Action Item:** Expect your world to have people with ironic behaviors and look for opportunities to learn and grow from what you see in them. *You can't buy a better education!*

When you consistently give that which you expect from others, life becomes much more fun. – Coach John S. Nagy

40. Avoiding Capture

Be okay with interrupting – especially when it's appropriate!
– Coach John S. Nagy

This letter was sent to me from a client:

Dear Coach!

I am tentatively scheduled to speak for an hour or so at a local business in a few weeks. The manager wants me to speak to a group about what led me to pursue my profession. I plan to talk about my training and give an elementary description of what is involved in the work I do and some examples of how my work is beneficial to my clients. I think I can include these things in my presentation and then open a discussion geared to the audience's personal interests. In addition, I will probably lead them through some exercises and I'm toying with the idea of doing a demo. I have two questions for you:

1. *How do you set & hold an appropriate boundary so that people don't go into deep & inappropriate sharing?*
2. *How do you handle a shy or non-participatory group?*

I would appreciate any support you can give me,

Signed: Avoiding Capture

– – – – – – –

Hi Avoiding Capture!

Wow! Your first question is about too much sharing and your second one is about not enough sharing! If you're looking for balance in your presentation, this is a great pair of questions.

These same two questions are often asked of me by my clients who, like you are about to do, deal with public speaking, business meetings or amazingly enough, even one-on-one encounters.

First, I congratulate you for making a commitment to get yourself in front of an audience. Do not take my kudos lightly. The fear of public speaking is more common than the fear of death so you're facing the bigger fear of the two here.

Let's tackle your first question: How do you set an appropriate boundary so that people don't go into deep and perhaps inappropriate sharing?

The first thing to do is personalize this. I have a sense that you're looking for some simple techniques to say "no." This is a good thing because there will be times when some person in your audience attempts to "get into your game, take control of your ball, and run with it." Your job, when this occurs, is to "wrestle your ball back" in a loving and gentle manner. This can be difficult to do, especially with those whom I call "hostage takers" because they go into long-winded monologues that hold you and the audience hostage.

If I were to restate your question more bluntly, "How do you interrupt a hostage taker without appearing to be as rude as the hostage taker?"

Whenever you provide an opportunity for an audience to interact with you, set your boundaries before you start anything else: Be specific with them (and yourself) about what kinds of information you're looking for and, more importantly, know when you're not getting that information. If you're asking questions, direct your questions very specifically and know when a respondent is not answering the questions. Some people will never answer a question directly and they take any question as permission to dump their own stuff on unsuspecting questioners.

174

Usually, they operate on the premise that they have to tell you all the background information in order for you to understand fully their response.

Learn to recognize that these are distractions. Your real challenge is to:

1. recognize when this is occurring (and if you're a public or private speaker, it will!)
2. have the courage to interrupt and re-direct them
3. do it!

When I am speaking to others, I often tell people that I reserve the right to interrupt them in order to continue moving the process along in the desired direction. If they tell me that they prefer no interruptions, then I ask them to contribute only when what they want to say is precisely in line with the end in mind. When they contribute things that don't support the end in mind, I have no problems with exercising my option to interrupt them.

A gentle interruption to remind them of our agreement often brings a smile from both the audience and the person you're reminding. I've actually had the sharing party thank me, and either summarize or stop entirely.

If I were to revamp my response to your original question, I'd say the best way to set and hold an appropriate boundary like the one you describe is to state that boundary clearly right in the beginning and have everyone agree to abide by it. This sets you and your audience up for only appropriate sharing and any interruptions you make will be perceived as gentle guidance rather than as rudeness.

Here's what I do at the beginning of most of my presentations where interactions are expected during the presentation. I first ask permission from the group to not waste any time and to allow me to be swift in moving through the topic. Because the topic will be moving so swiftly, some in the group may want to just observe so I also let them know it's okay to say "I'll pass!" to any question I might direct toward them. This way when I ask for a "yes" or "no" response from the participants, they also know in advance that other answers may be offered. I also let them know that further sharing from the group is okay as long as it stays on the specific aspects of the topic being discussed. If the sharing gets too detailed or moves off the topic, I reserve the right to interrupt to get it back on track. This technique works well and is a prime example of setting boundaries from the start.

The second question you asked was "How do you handle a shy or nonparticipating group?"

Let's "cut to the chase" on a long explanation here. First, understand that you don't "handle" anyone. All you can really do is offer things that may lead them, if they want to go in the direction you offer. Recognizing and accept this as a vital truth. This being said, there are several ways you can deal with a lack of response from an audience:

1. **Share Stories:** Have plenty of information in the form of interesting stories. Stories are a great way of saying it's "okay" to just sit back and listen. It's also a safe and warm way to invite your audience into a world you will create just for them.

2. **Invite Contribution:** At certain points in your stories, if you see someone whose body language shows that they want to say something, give them an opportunity, through verbal prompts, to affirm a "related-ness" to the story or to contribute something of their own. For example: *"Has anyone here ever experienced this situation?"* or, *"Who would like to share what happened to them?"*

3. **Plan Exercises:** Encourage audience participation through exercises. They're great "ice breakers." Use them throughout your presentation. Have a few ready in your back pocket you can bring out at "talking to a brick wall" moments. Your group may be looking for opportunities to interact with you or with each other. Provoke interaction by letting them try out some of what you present. They'll welcome any opportunity you offer.

I think you'll find these suggestions valuable and quite effective as you encounter situations like these in the future. Prepare for them by visualizing them in your mind's eye while practicing how you'd like to have these interactions go in the future. It'll work better for you if you do your visualizing practice sooner than later. Making this skill a part of your behavior means getting comfortable with it *now*.

Provoking Success! (Coach's Review, Recommendations, Questions and Unreasonable Requests)

1. **Action Item:** Establish boundaries up front in order to make them easier to maintain.

2. **Action Item:** When you do slip up and a hostage taker starts talking, give yourself permission to interrupt them and then do it. Most everyone will be grateful.

3. Respect the ways in which people want to participate.

4. **Action Item:** Provoke participation by giving them many opportunities.

5. **Action Item:** Visualize this now so you can have it become a part of you. (Enjoy! and have a Bodacious Presentation!)

When you establish, upfront, a boundary giving you permission to interrupt, your interruption of someone who is disrespectful of that boundary will be both expected and well deserved.
– Coach John S. Nagy

Uncommon Marketing

Effective marketing is about people knowing that you exist!
– Coach John S. Nagy

41. The Waving and Shaking Business

Most people consider the words 'marketing' and 'selling' to be synonymous. – Coach John S. Nagy

I've known some very good sales people who, despite their tremendous ability to sell, fail to bring in new business and do this quite *spectacularly*. You might say, "Coach, how can these people be "good" at sales if they fail to make the sale." I didn't say they failed to make the sale. Their closing ratios might well be near 100%. They may have a great ability to sell. Their personality or even their personal hygiene might be extremely attractive for the selling game. I said they fail quite *spectacularly* because of they are missing one critical ingredient in their business process that prevents them from reaching an agreement from the very beginning.

That crucial ingredient is knowing the differences between "what selling is" and "what marketing is." Although many people claim to know the difference between selling and marketing, most of them find themselves surprised by my spin on the differences. Knowing these differences empowers you to utilize these differences to work to your advantage!

Let's explore this and have some fun along the way.

Selling is all about the agreement. It is "shaking hands" and saying, "Okay, let's do this." It's all about:

- what's going to be agreed upon; how it's going to be carried out; who is doing the agreeing; when the agreement is to be negotiated and concluded; where the agreement is going to take place;

It may even include *why* these actions are taking place. It's all about coming to agreement on what is going to be exchanged between the buyer and seller based on needs or wants being met.

Marketing is all about telling people the agreement is available. It is "waving hands" (as opposed to shaking them) to get the attention of the people who could benefit. It's all about letting people know that there's an agreement out there for them to take advantage of that will meet a need or a want that they have. It's all about:

- What's available for agreement; who's making it available; where to get the deal; why the deal is so important to procure.

Marketing also includes being willing to give reminders from time to time to let people know that this agreement is still available for their benefit.

This outline of the differences between selling and marketing is simplified and incomplete. There are subtle things that could be added and they're not points that need to be understood here. The important question for you to ask yourself should be "What does this mean for me?" From what I've been exposed to in the professional world, there are many great sales people – few of them are true marketers.

Who are marketers? They're people who, among other things, know that they are the "best kept secrets" in any area where people can connect with them easily. Knowing this, they take all the actions necessary to get their secrets out to the right people for the right reasons. The secret: They can provide something of value to those who need what they have to offer. If potential customers do not know this, the provider is not known and hence a well-kept secret they are.

Do you want to succeed in having people know you are available? Then start the process by knowing the difference between selling and marketing. The following will help:

- Sales folk are good at showing you the advantages of closing the deal with them. Marketers are good at having the right people know that an advantageous deal is available.

- Sales folk can get you past objections and help you embrace the benefits of the deal. Marketers put the benefits right in front of you so that you will have no objections.

- Sales folk seek you out to make the deal (If they bang on your door or call you up, you're going to hear a pitch!) Marketers have you seek out the deal. (If you need something and know where to get it, the marketing was effective!)

So, what are you sensing here? Are you saying to yourself "Hey, wait a minute Coach, can't these two be worked together? The answer is "Yes." Can't I market in a way that sells too?" Well of course you can! The secret is knowing that you have to do *both*. If those who could benefit from your products or services don't know that you (and your products or services) exist, how can they make a deal with you? It's after they know and want it that you have opportunity to offer it.

For some sales folk, failure or mediocre success is inevitable. It's not that they can't sell. They may be very good at it. They just haven't put the word out as to what's available and whom they should contact. Without the critical ingredient of "waving hands," (getting people's attention) "shaking hands" (coming to an agreement) isn't going to happen.

Examples of marketing methods are varied. It might be in the form of articles published in local newspapers, trade journals and on the Internet. Another form may be speaking engagements for local clubs, charities or professional organizations. Yet another might take the form of "word of mouth" from people whom already have been provided that which you offer. Consider this: If your product has a logo and it is clearly visible to people other than those whom are using your product, you're marketing!

Marketing is all about getting attention. Did I provoke yours? Selling is coming to agreement. Don't you agree?

Provoking Success! (Coach's Review, Recommendations, Questions and Unreasonable Requests)

1. **Action Item:** Create a list of your marketing efforts.
2. **Action Item:** Answer the following questions:
   - How focused are each of your marketing efforts?
   - How focused do they need to be?
   - On a scale of one to ten, how effective are they?
   - What's missing to make it a perfect "10"?
   - How successful could you be if your marketing efforts were complimentary with your selling skills?
   - Do these questions apply to your business life or your professional life?
   - Might there be other aspects of your life where people don't know all of the great things you have to offer?

   You need to get someone's attention if you ever hope to come to any agreement. Have I gotten your attention?
   – Coach John S. Nagy

42. Scripts & Timing for the "Foot Challenged"

Whether you put your foot in your mouth or shoot yourself in the foot, the observer will always opt for another entertainer.
  — Coach John S. Nagy

Have you ever noticed how some folks seem to be totally devoid of feelings in their feet? You can always tell when you meet one of these unfortunate souls. Subtle things give them away. Things like the fully loaded machine gun locked on automatic, trigger pulled, with the muzzle placed squarely against their foot, for one. In addition, while the gun is unloading on their "under**stand**ing," because they have no feelings in their feet, they are oblivious to the disaster they're creating for themselves. As for the ones who put their foot in their mouth, I guess they like filet of sole. Moreover, it's just as hard to retain one's standing this way, too. We all recognize the telltale traits—lots of noise and mess; and we're the ones who are left feeling walked on.

The oddest thing about these folks is that many of them seem to succeed in spite of their ineptitude. The numbers are on their side. They forge ahead, regardless of their lack of awareness, and a number of sales still occur. No, a better word here is "happen"; sales still happen in spite of themselves.

I've coached a fair number of telemarketers and I've developed some good scripts with excellent teams to sharpen up their monologue to a fine edge. In all humility, I've created some mighty fine works of verbal art that have made Team Managers want to do the telephoning themselves, just for the experience of performing the script on some unsuspecting person who habitually answers their phone in spite of their caller ID display screams, "Don't do it!"

Now, I'm no different when it comes to playing telephone roulette, although unlike the average recipient of these audio assaults, I'm someone who has been on both sides of the telemarketing effort. This gives me an advantage and I find great fun in turning the tables on the very people I coach. That's just what happened for me one day.

It was a balmy Sunday morning, just a few minutes after nine, when I received the call. Everyone knows that Sunday mornings are supposed to be "sacred time." What sane person would want to disturb the typical American suburbanite in this time slot? Like almost everyone else, I dedicate Sunday mornings to personal time. Therefore, when the call came, I thought it must be an emergency and picked up.

"Hello, you've got the Coach!" The caller said, "Hello, sir, I'm calling to ask if you receive the *Times* newspaper."

I paused moment thinking, "What! This is not an emergency!" and quickly reframed my thoughts to "Ah ha! Opportunity! Let's see where this leads."

This person calling met the profile of a "numb foot." He hadn't taken the time to write a script that was right for the job. Logic says that you don't blind call someone who might already be receiving your product and then add insult to injury by calling them at an inappropriate time. If the person already receives your product, they will get a poor impression of the Company's marketers. Conversely, to increase sales without wasting resources, you should only call people who don't already receive your product. In addition, make your calls at a considerate time for that person.

Calling people during their "Sacred time" is a "no-no" when you want to start out on the right foot (and keep both feet in good standing). They will usually view a call like this as rude or worse, an assault. It will leave you struggling to make a connection with them and it will only succeed in annoying the person you're trying sell.

Back to our story: I thought, "Hey, now. This is *my* time and if I'm going to be disturbed, I'm going to make it worth it." I responded with a dramatically drawn out "IT'S NINE…O'CLOCK…IN THE MORNING!"

Not skipping a beat, the caller said, sarcastically, "Yeah, tell me about it!" To which I responded, "Great, I'm so glad you're up for it. Let me do just that... IT'S NINE…O'CLOCK…ON A SUNDAY MORNING! Are you SERIOUS?"

"Hey now, I don't like this either."

"Well, that should tell you something about what you're doing. If it doesn't taste right, spit it out and stop shoveling it in!"

Dead silence – it didn't really matter what occurred next, though I'll not leave you hanging on this – our parting was most amicable.

Mind you, I could have used my usual script when it comes to these calls. I could have cupped my hand over the phone to muffle it as I said, "You've reached the telemarketing answering device so please leave your name and number at the sound of the click." Sometimes that's just not as much fun on a Sunday morning.

When I get some poor telemarketer calling who doesn't have a clue, I take advantage of the moment to provoke some great material for educational stories. In this case, the caller executed some classic "foot shots" and created some great copy for me (and hopefully for you too!)

Provoking Success! (Coach's Review, Recommendations, Questions and Unreasonable Requests)

1. The words of a script as well as the way the words are delivered can make the difference between success and failure. *When* the script is delivered is equally important.
2. If you do the unacceptable, what you're selling had better be worth the social faux pas.
3. Good and bad reputations are created at two different speeds. Good ones take time; Bad ones take no time at all. They both have impact on sales.
4. **Action Item:** Research your audience before you make the call.
5. **Action Item:** Know the typical times your prospects would not want to be disturbed and avoid these times like a long tailed cat would avoid a rocking chair reunion.
6. If people already have what you're selling, you're wasting your time calling.
7. Sarcasm is always unbecoming and leaves a poor impression of whatever you are representing.

Coach's Note: *He who has been shot in the foot is usually unable to retain his standing, much less remain standing up. When you are the one who has done the shooting, please sit down and tend to your wounds – your understanding will thank you.*

Ring not church bells during business hours nor do business when church bells ring. – Coach John S. Nagy

43. Breaking through the Rejected Comfort Zone

Why would you want to invest in something you don't want?
– Coach John S. Nagy

A great many of my clients find that in order to reach goals they have set for themselves they have to extend themselves beyond their comfort zone on a regular basis. One of the ways they extend themselves is in the way they make cold-calls (contacting people they do not know). If you're like most people, making cold-calls is about as fun as having your teeth yanked out with pliers. My clients experience the same misery.

What most people don't realize is that they make cold-calls all of the time. We just don't realize it. We do it when we walk down the street and meet the gaze of people we encounter. We do it when we walk into a store to make a purchase for the first time. We even do it when we make a phone call to someone we don't know to ask for information we know they have. In principle, there is no difference in the process. There is on the other hand a difference in our *mind-set*.

In the previous examples, we are not invested in the *outcome*. We're invested in the *process*. The *process* of walking down the street will cause encounters with people. If we open ourselves up to meeting their gaze, we make contact. If we're not open, we don't make contact.

The same thing applies when we're making a purchase. We're not invested in a relationship between the storekeeper and ourselves. We're only invested in the *process* of making a purchase, if what they have to offer is what we want to buy.

Making a cold call over the phone is no different when we know that the person at the other end of the connection will do what they're supposed to do. "What's that?" you might ask. Think about the following: When you dial 1-411 (directory assistance), you expect the person who answers you to supply you with information you want. You invest yourself in the *process* of dialing the number while thinking about making the request. The only outcomes you can reasonably expect from the professional at the other end of the line is:

1. the information you seek

    or

2. the knowledge that the information is unavailable

The challenge with making a cold call is very much like when one person approaches another person for the first time, like at social gatherings and such. Often those who do the approaching have spent an inordinate amount of time and energy fantasizing about the *outcome* before they even begin to make their move. A lot of emotional letdown usually occurs when the fantasized expectations are not met.

We call this kind of *outcome* a poor return on investment.

To get a better *outcome* or a higher return on investment one must change their involvement in the *process*. The shift is easy and rewards are high.

Primarily, please understand I coach many sales professionals – from stockbrokers and investment advisers to attorneys and chiropractors. All of them are involved in sales to one degree or another and their professions require them to approach people they don't know. If they don't do this, their business pipeline dries up.

To prevent this, I ask my clients to take the same approach to cold calling as they would take when hiring personnel for their business. To hire people in the most effective and efficient way, one must *screen-out* potential employees rather than *screen-in*. The distinction between the two is simple. The former gives control to the employer. The latter gives control to the applicant. The same thing goes for cold calling. If you go into cold calling with the attitude that you are trying to screen people in, they will have control of the process. If you go into cold calling with the attitude of trying screen people out, you will have control. Ask yourself whether you would like to be in control or not in control of cold-calls. I'd venture to say that you'd opt for the former, just as most of my clients have done.

"Screening people out" gives you awesome power. It's energizing. It's relieving. It's empowering. Do you like how this sounds? Good! Let's provoke you toward creating a list of "to-dos" to make it occur.

The first item on the list: create the perfect "prospect profile." Put down in writing what qualities a person must have in order for you to do business with them. Any person you encounter who does not have these qualities is not a candidate for doing business with you.

The second item on the list: create a "reject profile." These include all the characteristics a person may have that would give you reason not to do business with them.

The third item on the list: commit these two profiles to memory *prior* to making the phone call. You'll want to have the assurance that you will be able to recognize any person you encounter as either a prospect or a reject. By having the two profiles memorized, you can quickly determine whether to invest yourself further in the process.

One of the neatest aspects of this method is that many people will voluntarily place themselves in the "reject" category without knowing it. People with the wrong attitude, low energy level, lack of interest, or poor civility place themselves in jeopardy of being rejected. They may be so far off target that it will become readily obvious to you that they don't make the grade. If you happen to be the recipient of screaming, rudeness, or bad language (designed to get you off the phone more quickly), their behavior merely tells you you've contacted a "reject." Once you're at ease with this process, you'll find humor in what used to feel like rejection, because you will have turned the tables and you will be rejecting *them* for all the right reasons.

Provoking Success! (Coach's Review, Recommendations, Questions and Unreasonable Requests)

1. **Action Item:** Identify the characteristics of the perfect candidate and the characteristics of the perfect reject.

2. **Action Item:** Write your two profiles out on paper.

3. **Action Item:** Commit these two profiles to memory.

4. **Action Item:** Make all calls and connections to screen-out, not screen-in – accept and reject appropriately.

5. **Action Item:** Invest yourself in the process not in the outcome.

Coach's Note: You'll find all of this applies to non-professional relationships too. Should you participate in relationships with a clear understanding as to what constitutes acceptable and unacceptable characteristics, the quality of the people you form and keep friendships with will improve dramatically. It's all part of the business of finding and keeping friends. Moreover, don't fool yourself into thinking you're the only one who knows this – high quality people already have their lists in place when it comes to how they view others, including you.

Invest in the process – especially one that will empower rather than frustrate you. – Coach John S. Nagy

44. Mind Set is Everything

A shift in perspective is life changing. – Coach John S. Nagy

Coach's Note: Here's another way to look at the same concepts presented in the " Breaking through the Rejected Comfort Zone" chapter with some difference in how you can apply them.

On the surface, this story will appear to be about telemarketing, so if that's your focus, it can help you in your business dealings. I've found another underlying theme in the story that has especially helped my single clients in their attempts to find and form relationships. Stay with me:

I sat in a client's office the other day and had the great fortune to witness his coming of age. He had asked me to sit in on a cold call session of his so he could benefit from immediate coaching feedback. During the first thirty minutes, I made my usual comments, "Stick to the script," and what I call the "SW4" mantra: "Some will, some won't, so what, someone's waiting, NEXT! I helped him clean up a few "uh"s, "ah"s, and "but"s, and fine-tuned some words and phrases. After twenty calls, I witnessed something grand. Until then, my client had been keeping score the usual way. He had annotated his list with scribbled comments about who was to be sent what mail-outs, when to connect with whom again, and who was "not interested." He'd done all this with some anxiety because he had anticipated that at any moment he could become emotionally drained from the process.

I, too, waited for a transition and not the one my client was anticipating. Through experience, I knew what would occur once he had really invested himself in the process.

On the twenty-first call, his actions completely shifted. I overheard the person on the other end say in a clear voice "I'm not interested." Rather than responding with the usual, "Okay" and hanging up, my client did something very special. He said "Thanks! I appreciate your honesty. Have a great holiday!" before he hung up. His voice quality was so perfect that I sat up in my chair. I recognized that the change within him was coming from a deeply sincere place inside him, and this is exactly what has to occur within you if you don't want to burn yourself out doing this task. He turned to his list and next to the person's name wrote, "REJECT." Then he went back over the list, struck out all the "Not interested" annotations and changed them to "REJECT." A look of amazing power came over his face, overshadowed only by his sly smile.

He had made a transition. Wanting to have a little fun with him, I asked what just provoked him toward these new actions. He reviewed it with me:

He'd suddenly realized, as he heard the last rejection, that this person didn't meet the criteria for doing business with him. When he saw that this person didn't make the grade, he became grateful for not wasting further time and energy on him. In that moment he decided to share a simple thank-you and wish him well before he got off the line. As he thought about it, he had felt a rush of energy came over him. He finally got it that the person at the other end wasn't rejecting him; *he* was rejecting the person at the other end. The call ended with a boost rather than a drain and a letdown.

As he hung up the phone, he placed the name in the appropriate location: the reject bin. There was no longer any need to put negative results down on paper. He decided to win by rejecting the name rather than hanging onto it as a failure.

It was great to see the glow in his eyes.

Provoking Success! (Coach's Review, Recommendations, Questions and Unreasonable Requests)

1. **Action Item:** Provoke yourself to know what you're truly looking for.

2. **Action Item:** Invest only in the process, not the outcome.

3. **Action Item:** Reject when there is no interest.

4. **Action Item:** If possible, share your gratitude, even if it's in silence or to a dial tone.

5. **Action Item:** Record *your* choices, not theirs. Even if they're interested, *you choose* to accept them for your next phase.

6. **Action Item:** Make your choices be choices that empower you.

7. **Action Item:** Stay in the game.

Coach's Note: *This concept is no different for personal situations. When you know the rules of the game, it's easier to play (and enjoy it too!)*

Focus is a choice; choose wisely. – Coach John S. Nagy

45. Waking Up to Find Them Leads

You can ask for referrals, but if you're referral-worthy, you won't have to. – Coach John S. Nagy

I tend to ask a lot of questions during meetings with clients. I like questions because they contain awesome potential and empower both the giver and receiver on many levels. Often times these simple conversations, sprinkled with these questions, can bring about some wonderfully entertaining growth experiences once the connection is made.

An example of this happened one day when a client asked me how to get more leads (potential customers). I told him that I'd love to get a discussion going and before we did, I wanted to ask him a few questions first. He reluctantly agreed, and again said that all he wanted from me was to learn how to get more leads. I agreed to tell him he if he'd just be patient. He unenthusiastically nodded his agreement.

I first asked him what he enjoyed most about his office environment. He said he enjoyed the amount of support he got from his coworkers. I asked him how many other financial professionals worked in his office. He said there were fifteen. I asked him, "Of the fifteen, how many would he say actually had a business plan?" The response was "About half of them." I then asked, "Of those who had a plan, how many were actually working it. He said, "About half of them."

I responded, "Great! You wanted to know how to get more leads, right?"

"Absolutely," he said, "but I wish you'd stop asking so many questions and get to it."

I told him the key lay right before him and he wasn't seeing it; he needed to listen more carefully to conversations – ours in particular. I said, "I'm a business coach. I'm always looking out for more potential clients, too. You've just told me that you know of fifteen other professionals in your office who could use varied forms of coaching support. The people without plans could use me to develop a business plan. The people with plans that were not working could use coaching support to get them back on track. The others who were left could use coaching support to increase their production or improve the return on their investments. Right?"

I was met with silence.

Smiling at him, I asked, "Do you get my point yet?"

He smiled back at me, put his chin to his chest and snickered, "That was so easy and I didn't even see it coming. Wow"!

"What's behind the 'wow!' you just shared?" I quickly asked.

He paused for a moment and then shared his thoughts with me. He had missed the most obvious of connections. All this time he was looking for a magic script to get referrals. He figured that if he did a good job, he'd get referrals. Until now, he hadn't made a connection that "plain old simple" conversation with his clients was great way of "breaking the ice"– *for his clients!* In turn, it helped his clients – his referral sources – come up with possibilities to check into.

He realized that no matter how good he is at doing what he does, he would only become "referral-worthy" when he helped *his clients* make their own connections.

I'm happy to report that he's provoking more connections these days.

Provoking Success! (Coach's Review, Recommendations, Questions and Unreasonable Requests)

1. **Action Item:** Find an area of questioning that solicits responses you know will bring you leads. This requires some knowledge of the person's background. I knew the client had co-workers. You could also focus on personal affiliations such as organizations, associations and clubs.

2. **Action Item:** At first, make sure the questions are as open-ended as possible. Practice the rule of thumb that the question should elicit something other than a "yes" or "no" response. A purist might add the requirement that this rule include any questions that could be answered with one-word responses.

3. **Action Item:** Use the questions to identify areas of comfort for the person talk. It's a lot easier to do this if you are genuinely interested in the person as an individual and not just as a source for information.

4. **Action Item:** Concentrate on making it easy for the person to share their connections with people they know. Use the questions to "guide" them through the process. Most people want to give leads to others just because they like your interest in them. You help them do this and they feel good about it.

5. **Action Item:** Once the conversation produces leads, get permission to contact them. If you do this respectfully, most people will actually make the introduction for you.

Coach's Note: *This* also *works well if you're looking to make more friendship connections. You'll be amazed at how much you can learn about a person if you only take a sincere interest in them.*

Insights amuse; revelations change lives. – Coach John S. Nagy

46. Time to Show Up

Some people learn just enough to get by and are shoved into the next grade just because they showed up. – Coach John S. Nagy

There's an old saying about "leading horses to water" that's been around for a while. Adages like this have staying power because there's so much truth behind them. Course facilitations I've done over the years perfectly illustrate this point. These courses always deal with helping people to add more value to their lives. For attendees, who are looking for the "big picture," their intent in taking the course also includes finding ways to add value to those people whom they encounter as they take their journey through life. Two recent courses I facilitated provided great examples of these two different, yet closely related intents.

The first course focused on creating and maintaining bonds with others. During the first class, I did my usual question asking— who were the attendees? What interests occupied their time? Where did they currently live? – and so forth. I intended these questions to give the class a chance to get acquainted and to give everyone a chance to share.

Some people didn't catch on to how important these introductions were. Those who didn't take the time to listen consciously to their classmates missed opportunities to gather information that would have assisted them in creating the very bonds they said they were looking to make. During these introductions, most people shared their personal and/or professional history, giving information about themselves that creates connections with others. In essence, these introductions are the beginnings of what could become friendships or partnerships – if the ball is not dropped from the start.

If you are serious about meeting people and forging bonds with them, there's great relevance to listening carefully. On average, each person you encounter has a sphere of influence that encompasses nearly 250 potential contacts. For even a small class of perhaps five people, we're talking about 1250 potential contacts – that's a lot of people!

After several introductions had taken place, I did a "reality check" to tell me who in the class had been paying attention. This really rattles any students who have not been consciously present. I asked the group to recap the previously shared information. Not one person could do it. The class' "body language" proclaimed that they were both un-engaged in the topic and somewhat irritated that I was seeking their enthusiastic participation.

Let me reiterate that we're talking here about a course of study intended to help the attendees create "friendships." It seemed ironic to me that the very thing these students thought they were looking for was something in which they were unwilling to invest.

Now, let's contrast this class with another class that occurred only a month later. I created the same setup for essentially the same topic. This time the class grabbed hold of the challenge — eyes lit up and smiles were passed during their sharing. The people attending were genuinely engaged and the strong bonding that resulted was unmistakable.

These people were both invested and investing! Wow, what a contrast!

The differences between the two classes didn't end there. At the end of the course, the first group left with very little interaction with each other or with me, as if they'd "put in their time" and that was enough investment. The second group couldn't have been more different. As their last class was ending, several members suggested that they keep in contact with each other to share how they were each progressing. Quite spontaneously, they circulated a list for names, phone numbers and email addresses. One member took on the task of getting the information out to the other members.

These people, in the second class, were totally committed and engaged in the subject at hand.

The evaluations of each class by its attendees were interesting, too. The responses of the first class were "flat line," written by people who were "not all there" during the class. One person wrote that he wished we could've covered some ideas on one particular aspect of the topic. If I hadn't introduced at least twenty ideas during our time on the subject, I would have written him a personal letter of apology. The truth is that he just was not consciously present during the class. I wondered where his attention had been focused and if it were possible that I might have been able to do to pull him back into the circle. Sadly, I doubted I could; connections can't be provoked in some cases.

The evaluations from the second class were very different. The participants wrote specific things that they planned to do to make a difference in their lives, both personally and professionally. In those same evaluations, they also shared the impact of the class on them and they even recommended others whom they thought would benefit from taking the course. These people were "living" the ideas we explored during that brief encounter.

That "horses & water!*" saying defined the first class. The attendees were there physically and not spiritually, emotionally and mentally. They had invested their time and only that for they really hadn't showed up at all.

I would not say the same thing for the second group. They left with warm feelings, knowing that there are people around who'll extend themselves for their own benefit and with a clear intent to benefit others as well. These group members were "present" for the class and most importantly themselves!

I recall another saying that could apply here:" 80 percent of life is just showing up." I'd have to agree that that's a key to having a worthwhile life. To do anything less is just "doing time."

Provoking Success! (Coach's Review, Recommendations, Questions and Unreasonable Requests)

1. What is your "end in mind" when you commit and engage yourself in an activity?

2. What do you have to *be* to *get* a new subject into your life? I deliberately chose the word "be" rather than "do." Why do you think I did this?

3. **Action Item:** Once committed to any activity, engage yourself in it as a full participant from the moment you start, even before the official start of the class.

4. Understand that nothing truly starts for you if you haven't committed yourself.

5. Know that the lesson has officially ended for you when you have chosen to invest yourself no longer in it, not when the instructor, tape, chapter or program ends.

6. To receive a return on your investment, you must first know how to invest. **Action Item:** Act and invest as if you are a person who is provoked to know the lesson of interest.

7. Without your heart, what you carry in your head is as dead as an unread book. How can your heart help you to carry your topic of interest more in your life?

* *"You can lead a horse to water but you can't make it drink."*

If you show up for something, make sure you're all there!
– Coach John S. Nagy

47. Business by Exception

Get butt-bit enough and you'll soon be sitting shorter.
– Coach John S. Nagy

Instructions that create the success you want should be followed without waver. It's not a terribly deep concept to grasp. If the results of following a good plan are there for everyone to see, it should be honored *without exception.* Why is this so important? Because making exceptions to "well thought out" plans, no matter how well intended, will cause problems in business success.

Even when people agree with this concept and know the problems that occur, sticking to a plan is often a challenge for some of them. Despite having a clear path, these people will do things that will *prevent* them from having an exceptional business (and for that matter, an exceptional life).

Let me explain why and make is personal too:

You may choose to go into business or you may accept a position within an already existing business. To succeed in that position, whether as owner/operator or as an employee, you must follow certain pre-determined standards to assure that the end-in-mind happens. Specific procedures need to be followed to uphold those standards during day-to-day operations.

If the system is designed well, by following these standards and procedures, you have success. Unfortunately, many people in business don't follow through on the very plans they've made. This is where the word "sabotage" comes in.

Let's reflect back for a moment. Do you remember the word "sabotage" from the "Wooden Shoes" chapter? It originated in Northern Europe where, according to legend, disgruntled workers threw their sabots, into the turning gears of a mill to protest poor management. "Sabots" are shoes made of hard, durable wood. The outcome of those grinding hard-wooden gears meeting those shoes caused all forward movement ceased. The mill stopped producing its intended output. The mill workers got the attention of the management; and we got the word "sabotage."

So what does this have to do with doing business by exception? Let's look at the concept of "being *done in* by exceptions," when your day-to-day (sometimes moment-to-moment) decisions don't line up with your purported, policy-driven choices. *Consider some examples of how these decisions might create sabotage*:

- You've been doing some cold calling and not found any prospects who meet your customer profile. In frustration, you find someone who doesn't quite meet your profile and you *decide* to lower your standards and your business process to accommodate this person so that they can do business with you.

- You have a client who doesn't follow through on their agreement with your company due to personal problems. In order to keep the client, you *decide* to adjust your standards and your contract to accommodate them so they will continue to do business with you.

- You really want to have a relationship or at least a connection with someone and you are not inspiring their interest. You *decide* to modify your standards and normal practices so you can provide them with something you don't normally offer in order to create an interest in you.

You might say that in all three cases these exceptions were necessary to move the process forward. Actually, the fact is that the process was already doing just fine producing the results it was designed to produce. The problem wasn't with the process; it was with your *decision* to over-ride the screening out capabilities within the process. In the first example above, a process existed to screen out unsuitable prospects. If you, the cold-caller, decide to make an exception, then the process must change in order to accommodate the new customer, along with the profile of any other potential prospects. Result: The operator no longer controls the process. The customer now controls it.

With the loss of control comes an outcome most people in business dread: "The High Maintenance Back End." This occurs when you make an exception to the process to allow for the servicing of those who, according to the original design and intent of the process, were not intended to be serviced. The time required to shift and to recreate the process so it can accommodate the new customer takes away from the time required to service the process itself.

Another way of saying this is that the process now controls you. This condition continues until you invest your time, energy, and resources to rework the process so it can run by the new set of procedures, including the changes you have made. In the meanwhile, until the reworking is done, you have to service any *unplanned for* new customers who have *new requests* which your system is not currently designed to handle. If you can summon enough energy to maintain this new process, all its patrons, and still enjoy your life, you're a better person than most.

Once you have made an exception to your process, that precedent opens the door to other exceptions that ultimately create a time, energy, and money sponge. A sponge is something that sucks things up and requires additional resources and effort to get a return and the return is never 100% of what was given in the first place. Classic examples of money sponges are assets that depreciate over time. They require huge amounts of dollar support to keep them maintained – most cars, trucks, house trailers, ink jet printers, and of course, gold diggers, are a few examples. In the case of our story, making an exception requires you to make further investment in reinventing the process rather then in merely maintaining it. Your original investment to develop your process may have given you little return and because of the exception you made to this process, you now must invest even more in the process.

Similarly, the second situation above, in which the client fails to follow-through on the agreement, calls to mind other sponges. You are required to invest time to either change your process or (possibly) to hold this person accountable for their actions– if they are willing to let you do this. Then you must invest more energy and more of your other resources to be able to do this – energy and resources that would not be necessary if the follow through had occurred or if you hadn't change your game plan. You must also personally invest your spirit in this modification of the process – your emotions, thinking, and planning. Moreover, you must make shifts in your usual way of doing things in order to accommodate the new situation.

When you *decide* to make an exception, the customer gains control of your process. The problems that occur afterward cannot be anticipated because your process was designed to accommodate different conditions. The snowball effect eventually produces more problems until the avalanche can be heard three states away. If clients don't honor their agreements with you – regardless of the reason, sound or otherwise, – they are no longer candidates for your products or services. Your process require specific agreements be honored. Until clients meet the requirements for doing business with you, they are better off doing business with another provider.

I know this sounds tough. Most successful business processes have been honed from experience and a well-thought out plan. When you look honestly at the times you've made an exception to your process – especially when you knew better – what percentage of the time did the results end up in your favor?

Please remember to take into consideration all the sponges that came into existence during the cleanup effort afterward. Sure, the outcome might have ultimately moved your business in another direction, but was that movement well thought out, or did it drag you along while you hoped and prayed that you'd made the right decision? I have seen a lot of this inadvertent movement in business today.

The last of the three situations presented above presents the personal side dealing with people by making exceptions. You *decide* to offer something you normally don't to keep a person's interest. More times than not, everyone involved feels drained and ultimately all are left with sore spots in their hearts.

This has little difference from the situation where a decision is made to bring someone into your process who doesn't meet your profile. No matter how well intentioned, the outcome is generally a disaster. Personal processes and behaviors rarely change. Once an unsuitable person comes into another's process, they soon discover the process can't accommodate both their needs. As each person invests, "hoped for" results rarely come to fruition. The return-on-investment is less than that which they invested. Sometimes accusations of deceptions and hidden agendas further muddy the water. One or both parties leave feeling empty, angry or hurt. These are but symptoms of the actual cause – making exceptions.

Doing any business by exception, whether personal or professional often demands unnecessary expense and drainage. If opportunities attempt to provoke you out of your plan, consider passing it up. Lucrative exceptions must be well thought out and accompanied by a willingness to create a new process which will accommodate changes these opportunities require.

Coach's Note: *This topic can provoke many hours of great and deep conversations when applied toward spiritual matters.*

Provoking Success! (Coach's Review, Recommendations, Questions and Unreasonable Requests)

1. Know your process well enough to make decisions that support it fully.

2. **Action Item:** Commit to the process without exception. Changing the rules in mid game changes the whole structure of the game and its outcomes.

3. Opportunities may arise in which an exception seems appropriate. Any exception to a well thought out process must be well thought out *before* it occurs.

4. Risk management means doing all you can to increase the probability that outcomes will be in your favor.

5. A "High Maintenance Back End" which brings little return on investment is a signal that your process is running you and not the other way around.

6. **Action Item:** Create a list of past "exceptions" you've made and write out the lessons you believe were presented for you to learn. How did your behavior change for the better as a result?

7. **Coach's Note:** *Not all exceptions are negative.* What exceptions have you made in the past that actually added "value" to your process? How did they set a precedent for better returns into the future? How did these exception differ from the ones that cost you? What is the vital difference?

If you want exceptional results, personal or otherwise, make sure your processes are not governed by continuous exceptions that redirect you and force you to rewrite your plan.
– Coach John S. Nagy

Uncommon Sales

Selling is about coming to agreement. No agreement, no sale.
– Coach John S. Nagy

48. What's your FAB?

Sales rule of thumb: know the benefits that your service or product will give your client and share them first.
– Coach John S. Nagy

Most sales training seminars emphasize how important it is to share the benefits of a product or service with a potential client, yet many trainers give examples that have nothing to do with benefits and everything to do with positioning the prospect to benefit. They don't get it that there's a big difference between positioning someone and benefiting them

I occasionally talk about this subject when I'm coaching and find a lot of confusion between the two. I'm embarrassed to say that I've even contributed to that confusion in the past. Fortunately, since then I've been graced with the following acronym: FAB (Features, Advantages, Benefits). FAB creates a nifty way to keep track of the "benefit thing" and work it into your business so you can help your clients make connections that count.

Most people in business have been advised, "Features tell, stories sell," a strong point to consider when you're attempting to improve your income stream. Knowing the difference between features and benefits could mean the difference between a huge inventory backlog (the technical phrase is called "Inventory Stipation") and inventory that is moving.

Even more important, you need to know the difference between **advantage** and **benefit**. Let's look at these differences in simple terms by using the "story of the blue ballpoint solution" to illustrate the points:

A company is continually having a problem in their document department. The copying machines create replicas that are almost indistinguishable from the originals. Because of this, the department staff is faced with mounting losses of their original documents because the originals are frequently being given away rather than the duplicates. When copies of copies of copies are made, each succeeding replica, although *almost* indistinguishable from its predecessor, is of slightly lower quality. This is known as document degradation.

The ideal solution for this problem is to have some inexpensive and quick way available to differentiate an original from a copy. One vehicle for doing so is to make sure that all original documents are signed in blue ink because the signatures on the duplicate copies will appear black. (Admittedly, I could flower this story up a whole bunch with added drama – people getting upset, losing jobs, corporate espionage, romance, legal briefs, etc. I believe this is not needed for a very simple example.)

Let's look at the distinguishing elements of the story:

Feature: "Blue" – The pen has blue ink as a feature.

Advantage: "Tool" – The use of this blue ink pen helps the users tell the difference as to which document is the original and which one is the photocopy. The advantage only gives information and no "hook" to a potential user.

Benefit: "Assurance" – The user knows which document is a copy, which is an original and has no confusion on this issue anymore. The benefit is having certainty without confusion and no chance for document degradation. Benefits give the "hook." *It makes it personal.*

Notice what's really occurring here. The advantage actually "positions" the end user to receive and experience the benefit, i.e., the desired result. The benefit itself is the emotional anchor (called the "hook" or "anchor" in some circles). It puts the potential end user in a place where they are provoked toward seeing, hearing, or feeling the use of the product, and they *like* what they are feeling – hence the "anchor."

Next time you are promoting your products, services or interests, you might want to consider emphasizing the story aspect as shared above. This has everything to do with positioning the end user so that they experience that emotional anchor long before the product or service is even delivered.

Coach's Note: *Can you imagine how provoking this would be to your success if you used these insights in setting up your goals, making your plans and living your life? What **benefits** can you imagine and create for yourself to invest yourself fully in your desired path?*

Provoking Success! (Coach's Review, Recommendations, Questions and Unreasonable Requests)

1. The end-users must connect emotionally with the experience of your product, service or interest for investments to occur.
2. Your products, services or interests will sell themselves if you present them right *and* if they're right for the prospect.
3. FAB
   a. **F**eature: e.g., Blue
   b. **Ad**vantage: e.g., Visual Cue
   c. **B**enefit: e.g., More Emotional Certainty
4. **Action Item:** Answer the next two questions:
   a. What great benefits can you imagine for yourself to make this work in the personal realm?
   b. How can you create them and do this soon?

People invest to benefit, so let them know what the benefits are. Then they will invest themselves. – Coach John S. Nagy

49. Look What THEY Did for Me!

Under-promise, over-deliver. Who gets excited over getting only what they asked for? Gratitude's good but excitement is what builds client loyalty best. – Coach John S. Nagy

One day, I traveled with a client onto the road of "getting new customers." My client was attempting to build a customer base and wanted to know the easiest way to do it. My response was, "It depends on the business."

My client really hated my "winging" a short response his way and asked me to clarify what I said.

I started to explain my response and halted in midstream. I said, "Have you ever had anyone come up to you and say something like 'Look what **they** did for me!' with a heavy, excited emphasis on 'they'"? My client sat back and reflected a moment before he responded, "Boy! That's a tough one. I can't really recall that happening to me."

That's precisely what must be overcome. Most people respond the same way as my client did. For the most part, products and services in this country are provided to people to satiate "needs." The result is that the end user walks away "satiated" and quite silent in their contentment. They got what they expected; their needs were met and that's about it.

Occasionally you may run across someone who didn't have many expectations in the first place. You can spot them easily. They're the ones with the somewhat bewildered "Are you sure I was supposed to get all this for such a small fee?" look. They walk away as if they'd paid for a guppy and received a trout. Some of them catch on that it was a sweet deal and smile in delight, joyfully spouting, "Look what I got!" as they continue on their way. They may brag about the deal to a few others. The

211

transaction realizes little else for your business except the possibility of a repeat customer.

Coach's Note: *Be sure that they know that you know what you gave them. There's only a slim chance of them becoming repeat customers if they think they outsmarted you and got away with it.*

The sad thing is that's *all* many businesses hope for, believing that the level of service and product they provide will create customers for life. While this may keep a business steady, it won't actively promote or grow a business.

If *you* want to break out of the "same old business" rut and have your business soar, you have to provoke yourself toward doing for your clients what others in your field are not. You have to get your clients to *both* spout with delight *and* squeal with glee. You do this by making sure you deliver far beyond what is expected by your clients and far more than what you promised.

This is why I asked my client, "What do you hear your clients say about you to others? Do you hear 'Look what **they** did for me!' from them?"

Let's step back from this narrow view and apply it to a much wider field. Please consider the notion that everyone is your customer (a.k.a. "client") in some way. Treating everyone you know and deal with in this manner opens up many doors that would otherwise remain closed. If you're looking to create broader loyalty and greater potential for more relationships outside your present ones, you might want to examine this manner more closely.

Provoking Success! (Coach's Review, Recommendations, Questions and Unreasonable Requests)

1. Satiation = Silent Contentment ("_____")

2. Delight = Joyful Talk ("Look what I got!")

3. Glee = Rejoicing Song ("Look what **they** did for me!")

4. **Action Item:** Answer the following questions:

   - If you had to choose from one of the above, which do you think would produce the most inquiries about your product or service, and in fact have interested parties hopping out of the woodwork?

   - What do you need to add to your business process to produce gleeful customers who sing your praises long after the transaction is finished? (CAUTION: Answering this question may mean the difference between silently satisfied clients – along with a huge prospecting/marketing bill – and customers who are your *best* promoters!

   - How can you apply this paradigm outside your normal business focus?

   Position your clients to experience true 'glee'!
   – Coach John S. Nagy

50. Good Looking

It's not what you're thinking; it's how you're thinking.
– Coach John S. Nagy

When I ask people if eye contact is important, many agree that it is. I hear from them that eye contact helps in forming, building and maintaining relationships. They include in their sharing that *how* eye contact is made strongly indicates how people are related to each other. The timing of glances, staring, focus and blinks all affect the quality of communication too. It fascinates me how much can be communicated by our eyes.

I've studied eye contact and motions enthusiastically over the years ever since I was seventeen and an equally young lady friend told me her father didn't trust me. I was at a total loss as to what I could have done to earn such mistrust from a man with whom I'd had very little contact so I asked her why.

She said that he'd been taught that anyone who didn't look him in the eye was not to be trusted. Since he hadn't seen me looking him in the eye, he concluded that I couldn't be trusted. I found his rationale confusing, as it didn't match my self-image at all.

I had been raised in a culture where young people only looked in the eyes of equals. We were taught to treat anyone older or socially superior—for example, a parent of a friend – with respect. That meant giving a momentary glance of eye contact to telegraph that we were listening to them and then turning our glance downward to show our respect for their position.

The only time we made total eye contact with a superior was when they insisted that we look them straight in the eye. This was usually done as both a sign of our respect for them and as a means of intimidating us during an interrogation.

Of course, when my friend told me of his father's mistrust, I realized that I had a lot of reprogramming to do.

Since then, I've kept an "ear" open for the reasons people avoid eye contact. The primary reason people give seems to be a lack of self-confidence. Other reasons I've heard have been 1) discomfort, 2) deceit and, 3) (one that escapes many) habit.

I would invest in the self-confidence theory if it had more credibility. I've seen too many people, whom I know are self-confident, fail the eye-contact test (it's part of the self-confidence theory) for other reasons. I'm aware that the self-confidence theory does hold relevance for some situations. In the cases with which I'm familiar, it rarely applies. More often, I've noticed that people tend to be "eye-contact challenged" as the result of latter three.

These three, and probably more, affect our readiness to engage our eyes with another. Yet, professionals who seek to inspire direct eye contact continue to cite "lack of confidence" as the culprit that prevents visual engagement. The poor souls who hear this misguided advice walk away feeling more confused than clear, even to the point of feeling guilty and ashamed. They might start to believe that they lack self-confidence. Who knew? Of course, they don't lack self-confidence at all; the well-meaning trainer simply didn't know that there were other reasons for not making eye contact.

I believe well-entrenched habits are the single greatest influence on lack of eye contact. Unfortunately, I can't say to someone, "Just look 'em in the eye!" when they ask me for a solution. It doesn't work that way. Old habits die hard and eye-contact-challenged people face an uphill battle if they try to squelch old habits by force.

Instead, I recommend increased awareness. I ask my clients to focus their awareness on where their eyes are looking at any given moment when they are with others. Improving awareness is the beginning of a solution.

Another part of the solution is **not** to beat yourself up (self-shaming, chastisement, and castigation are all ways to beat yourself up) if you find your eyes are not where you think they should be. The fact is your eyes are always where they should be, because they are where your mind is focused. If your eyes are not where your thoughts are, you have a bigger problem.

Most people think because their eyes are not focused on what they *pre*-conceive as appropriate, they are doing something wrong. They typically feel guilty, which engenders an ill-conceived internal dialog designed to "discipline" them into submitting to the desired behavior. They punish themselves for "improper eye behavior" rather than looking at the thoughts that got them there in the first place. In other words, unsuccessful people focus on the effect and not the cause.

If this is your situation, provoke yourself toward exploring the cause of this. Make whatever adjustments you need to communicate more effectively for yourself and with others. Your results will be most bodacious!

Coach's Note: *Rather than berating themselves, successful people construct an internal dialog that rewards them for the improved awareness of their focus and a gentle redirection of their focus toward the desired end. They find the causes and work with them, rather than futilely pushing away the effects.*

Coach's Bonus: *Know your "eye etiquette." Many people don't realize that "eye shuttling" holds an important place in eye contact protocols. Eye shuttling shows respect for the other party and gives "eye breathers" to all involved.*

Shuttling entails glancing away momentarily, then returning focus to allow the other person to do the same. People who maintain constant eye contact and fail to practice this gentle rhythm of back-and-forth glances come across as rude. On the other hand, people who shuttle in a staccato manner often come across as if they are hiding something. If a person doesn't know and respect the shuttle game, the encounter or relationship can end uncomfortably.

Provoking Success! (Coach's Review, Recommendations, Questions and Unreasonable Requests)

1. If you find yourself staring somewhere else, ask yourself why the person you're with is less important than what you're focusing on.

2. Understand why you are not engaged in the conversation and relating to the other person: Where are your thoughts at the instant? Are you numbing out and waiting for the interaction to be over? Do you have a higher priority that you need to take care of so you will then be freer to interact with the person in front of you?

3. **Action Item:** Practice "Eye Shuttling"

4. **Action Item:** Reward yourself when you see your awareness is working.

Coach's Note: *It takes thirty days to establish a new behavior and ninety days to entrench it. This means you are probably going to fail at least once during the first thirty days as you work toward your goal. The people who succeed are those who praise themselves for being aware of their shortcomings rather than beating up on themselves for not succeeding immediately.*

Your eyes always say so much more than your words do.
– Coach John S. Nagy

51. Getting Out of the Way

Allow others the opportunity for growth by letting them face their struggles. – Coach John S. Nagy

A talk with one of my clients brought back a reminder of what I had learned early on about the helping professions. We're often staffed by compassionate people who sometimes get too caught up in the struggles of others. My client's situation was a typical case. She told me that she had ended an interview with a prospective client because she had concluded that her prospect would be uncomfortably stressed if he took advantage of her services.

I wasn't surprised, for I used to do the same thing until I discovered that I was letting my personal opinions override what I was there to do – provide the people I serve full information regardless of what I thought of the stress created by their situation. It's a lesson we pay for dearly and one I could see that my client needed to learn too.

I inquired further into her reasoning. She said that if a prospect was obviously stressed by taking advantage of her services, she stopped the information flow. She saw no reason to provide the remaining information to the prospect so he could make an "informed" decision. Her rationale for her decision was filled with well thought out compassion but she was missing a critical piece: When she decided that the prospect shouldn't take advantage of her services, she had made a decision for him. She had chosen to withhold the remaining options; she had surmised that any of those options would very likely cause the prospect to experience some hardship. In essence, she had taken away from him his ability to make the choice for himself.

A professional's character and purpose are tested in situations like this. What is offered may seem to be antagonistic to our clients' best interests (or what we believe are our clients' best interests). Frequently we believe that we are being called upon by a higher purpose to decline giving our services due to our perception of the anticipated struggle it might cause our clients. At other times, we may have a sense that the time is not right for providing services. During situations like these, the very essence of each professional is tested, whether we want to admit it or not.

In these moments, I want to believe that our best intentions are carried out. Sometimes it's just not always possible to be clear as to what's best for our client or even what the underlying truth of the situation is. What might begin as "heart warming" service to others can become a "heart wrenching" exercise for us. It doesn't matter how many times we consciously work to prevent this. Doing business is like doing life: we will often see the struggles of people who are called upon to make life-changing choices. As professionals, we need to be invested in a process that helps guide them through their selections. We should not be invested in their eventual path until their path actually involves us.

"Why shouldn't we be invested in that eventual outcome?" you might ask. This is a great question to ask and here's my response:

We may think that their selection runs counter to their best interests, so we decide to "help" them by withdrawing offers that might cause them distress, forgetting that those same offers might be the very lifeboat they need – uncomfortable as it might be. By doing this, we have invested in their future. We might attempt to influence it *because of our discomfort, not theirs.* How ironic that our well-intentioned compassion can get in the way of giving others the assistance they actually need.

I've coached many professionals who provide services designed to assist and perhaps alleviate conditions that would otherwise grow worse. Yet the very cost of the service often causes additional stress and even hardship in the short term, much to the client's dismay. Just as often, professional service providers may be so moved by their clients' situations that they decide to **avoid** pursuing getting commitments because of the professional's own inability to deal effectively with personal discomfort.

As a business coach, I could make decisions for my clients that wouldn't require them to go beyond their comfort zone. I could avoid pressing issues that would cause them discomfort. I could also be fired for *not* pressing those same issues, because that's what they hired me to do. The moment I fail to expect from my client what they want for themselves is the moment I fail them as a professional. I'm in their lives for the express purpose of supporting them to break through the confines of "comfort."

When I look at the big picture, in every case, regardless of my input, clients ultimately choose for themselves – no matter what I believe to be my persuasive abilities. I'm asked along for the adventure, but if I throw in personal decisions based on my judgment of their situation, I'm not doing them justice. My job is to reflect back to them what I see as their struggle, advise them on what I see as available alternatives, and help them stay clear on what they are selecting. This includes the commitments they are making contrasted with what I perceive they can comfortably take action on. Just because I believe a person will become uncomfortable at a certain point doesn't mean I need to step in to prevent that discomfort. Discomfort, or even outright pain, has many reasons; some never expressed and some needing to be faced.

Many consultants and sales professionals get themselves in a bind by prejudging their clients and prospects as unable to rise to the occasion. They fail in their tasks because they don't provide or even advise their clientele of available options. Somewhere along the line, they decided for their clients or prospects and stopped doing what they'd been requested to do: share how to get to the next level of success. Provoking next level activity generally means breaching one's usual comfort zones to meet the challenge.

This can't occur if we attempt to do the deciding for them.

After our conversation, my client realized that it was in everyone's best interest to be fully informed and accept that this might include additional stress. She no longer wanted to assume that she knew what supporting structures were or were not in place for her prospects until they'd heard the complete presentation. Then *they* could choose for themselves.

I asked her to go all the way through her future presentations, regardless of any perceived stressors, keeping in mind that people will often do amazing things when they believe their needs will be met.

Coach's Note: Just in case you believe this writing might be counter to creating "maintenance free" relationships, professional or otherwise, keep in mind that *process* is still important and if the prospect doesn't meet specific criteria, this should over-ride the option to continue. Your process should always include this. If you're swayed to withdraw because of *your own inability to deal with the discomfort to the prospect, think twice.* If the prospect meets specific criteria, allow them their struggle – d*on't get in their way.*

Coach's Point to Consider: *How can you apply this to your personal relationships? If you're tempted to intervene for friends or loved ones, take a moment to examine your motives. Step away if your discomfort is driving your actions. Keep in mind that it's their struggle – not yours!*

Provoking Success! (Coach's Review, Recommendations, Questions and Unreasonable Requests)

1. How often have you made a personal decision that took away another's opportunity to stretch their wings because of discomfort *you* felt about the situation?

2. **Action Item:** When you're uncomfortable with others' struggles, resist attempting any rescue that would prevent them from facing the challenge before them.

3. Often, the best action to take is to present all available options that help to move people toward accomplishing their goals.

4. **Action Item:** When someone else's discomfort moves you to want to decide for them, remember: It's their opportunity to struggle not yours.

5. **Action Item:** The greatest gift we can give others is to believe that they can rise to the occasion even when all indications appear to the contrary. Believe!

6. **Action Item:** People will surprise you every time, if given the chance. *Give them the chance.*

"Butterflies that haven't struggled from their chrysalis are crippled by lack of stress and hence die." – *Coach John S. Nagy*

52. That "Fiercely Independent" Attitude

Fierce independence demands a high price.
– Coach John S. Nagy

An old timer shared with me a conversation that he'd had with a newcomer. It seems that the newcomer had complained to him that he hadn't made as many sales as he'd hoped for. The old-timer shook his head in disgust and asked the newcomer, "How many Office Support calls have you made in the few weeks you been out banging on doors?"

The newcomer's response that triggered the old-timer's disgust – "Well, er, uh... ...none."

It's understandable why the old timer shook his head. It's just as understandable why the new guy failed to be as productive as he could be. That "fiercely independent" attitude he was sporting was showing its ugly side. He hadn't been taking advantage of his organization's support system, so, one after another sales opportunities had slipped through the cracks of the newcomer's "lone wolf" system.

The newcomer was not working from a team approach and "Teamwork" is why you have "Office Support." This specific support system is designed for everyone, experienced or not. Old timers know this and use the system to their advantage, often going so far as to use other old timers as their personal team members. They know that they can depend on their team members to supply support when and where it's most needed.

This makes sense. There's something very powerful about picking up the phone in front of a prospect, making contact with a perceived expert on the other end of the line, and having that second party speak with the prospect. The prospect gets several positive impressions:

- They have an immediate connection to a large, well-established company.
- That company cares about prospective buyers and its employees.
- If the individual sales person doesn't know something or can't help with a need, there are other resources quickly available on the phone or online.

Sometimes this sort of connection is precisely what they need, especially if they've been experiencing any doubts about the company's existence or validity. New clients who are already on-board experience the same impact during "new clients' registration" type follow-ups. They get to see that there are more people supporting them than just the one representative sitting in front of them. Another positive powerful aspect of teamwork is what it can do for the representative who is asking for assistance. The support team can keep the prospect occupied while the rep recharges, rethinks, detaches, observes, and regroups – exactly what he needs in order to get back into the game with his batteries recharged. Old timers sometimes think of it as a tag team operation - a simultaneous tandem effort at accomplishing a goal. Some have even used it for dramatic effect to accomplish what they'd have had to work harder at doing by themselves. Variations on this theme are endless, as the well-practiced game-play helps to get the prospect what they really need.

Old timers deserve the title of "winner" by virtue of still being in the game. They use all the equipment they're given and they have learned to rely on a "team" to help them. They understand that leaving any gear unused because of an unwillingness to work with a team often "drops the ball" on possible wins.

Veterans are not willing to accept losses they could have avoided. Instead, they use the team approach to increase or leverage their successes and the successes of their prospects. That advantage doesn't occur with a "fiercely independent" attitude. The solo effort misses what a team can offer.

Yes – you don't always have to use the team. For the times that really count, why not let the system support your success in every way possible? What do you have to gain?

Coach's Note: *If you're unfamiliar with having a team to support and work with you, try seeking out an old timer who already has your trust and respect and ask to be part of his or her team. You'll have the opportunity to watch a pro at work and you'll get a better idea of what your own strengths and weaknesses are.*

Here's a provoking point to ponder: *If you think this chapter applies only to receiving help, think again. People often benefit most by giving back what was given to them. In this way, they position themselves to sharpen their skills by teaching these skills to others. Consider this: What might you gain if you were the mentor or guide on someone else's team?*

Provoking Success! (Coach's Review, Recommendations, Questions and Unreasonable Requests)

1. Whom have you identified as part of **your** team? Are you part of a team or apart from a team?

2. What might cause your reluctance to use them? What might cause your reluctance to be of help to a team member in need?

3. What opportunities can you envision where your team is used effectively? Can you envision yourself as being used effectively on a team?

4. What are some different ways you can involve your team players to help improve your presentation to your advantage and to benefit of your prospects? Can you be open to others involving you to leverage their presentations to advantage?

5. **Action Item:** Identify times you could have used your team to help you move into your future.

6. How might not having a team or not being part of a team be holding you back?

Interdependence is the backbone of abundance.
– Coach John S. Nagy

Uncommon Coaching

Coaching comes in many forms. – Coach John S. Nagy

D. Coaching Basics

Good discussions 'shake out' what's really needed.
— Coach John S. Nagy

I had an interview one day with a man who owned a local financial advisory firm. He had been referred my name through a business friend who recommended that he contact me for coaching. As the conversation unfolded, it became apparent that he had the typical challenges most small business owners have – time crunches, poor delegation, few systematic or automated approaches, marketing inconsistencies and financial tightness, among others.

At one point in our chat, he posed a question to me. "John, if you're not a CFP, Series 7, 63, CPA or trained in some way in the financial field, how in the world are you going to be of help to me?"

I paused a moment, knowing the answer to the question, then gave him a firm friendly glance and a question in return, "Do you have a clear picture of where you want to take your business?"

He looked a bit uneasy as he replied "Well, somewhat."

I had spent enough time with him to feel comfortable with firing back "Do I have your permission to be brutally inquisitive with you for the next five minutes?"

He smirked back at me with anticipation. "Sure, why not?"

"May I be equally blunt if your responses could be different?"

He again nodded an affirmative. His face took on a curious demeanor.

"Good," I said and asked him the typical opening question I give to most business owners who are considering taking on a coach, "What do you do for a living?"

He looked noticeably relieved at the question and said "Gosh, that's an easy one. I was expecting a tougher one. Basically, I'm a financial professional who gives advice and related support to my client base."

I said, "Good start. Now brace yourself! I don't think you're quite on target. I'm going to be bold here so tell me if this would be a more accurate answer: You're a business owner who has chosen to personally provide financial services and products to a specific target market and as a result created a job for yourself."

He blinked. Then he blinked again and started to stare off into space for a moment. The contemplative expression changed to one of recognition. He grinned and said, "Ya know, that's the problem I'm having. I'm stuck *doing* my business and as a result, I don't own it anymore. It owns me."

"Great, then what's the first thing you need to focus on so you can break this pattern?"

"That's a good question. What would you recommend?"

Not wanting to get into 'advice mode' just then, I replied "How 'about telling me who you are, coupled with where you want to go, because I can tell that what you're doing now isn't supporting you in achieving what you want in your life."

"You're right there, Coach." he replied. "I don't have anywhere near the time to do the things that need to be done, much less time to do the things I want to do, that this job is supposed to be supporting."

"Let me ask you this," I said, "if money wasn't an issue, and you sincerely want to have this practice prosper, what would you put in place to get to the next level?"

"Wow. I think I'm getting a better idea why my friend referred me to you. I just answered my own question about your lack of financial credentials. You don't need them to coach me. You're focusing on the business aspect and not the financial services aspect. Okay I got it now." The conversation ended with his scheduling a formal coaching session.

He "got" that a good coach didn't need to have the technical credentials of the client. Instead, a coach needs to know "business" and human beings well enough to co-create an environment that moves the client forward. In this case, we worked together so the client could safely challenge his comfort zone and focus on creating what he really wanted in his life.

As a result, he arrived at the answer very quickly. He "got" that I could provide the support he needed to grow and that the issue of "my financial credentials" was not an issue at all.

He has continued "getting" more from his coaching relationship over the years. At the time of this writing, he's grown his practice far beyond what he had originally imagined. It now includes two other partners as well as assorted assistants. The projected figures for this year's end look like he's once again going to surpass his projected growth.

I've been honored to be part of the team that provokes him!

Provoking Success! (Coach's Review, Recommendations, Questions and Unreasonable Requests)

1. **Action Item:** How do you see your business and life performing into the future?

2. **Action Item:** On a scale from one to ten, with ten being "great," how well do you see yourself currently running your business? How about your life?

3. If your answer is less than a ten, what would you have to add to make your business a perfect ten? How about your life?

4. If your answer was a perfect ten, then what does the next level of success look and feel like for you in business or in life?

5. **Action Item:** What must you commit to do in order to make this next level occur for you and as quick as possible?

Coach's Note: *If your interest is provoked enough to want to,*

- *take a coaching "test drive" or*
- *look at some challenging coach-type questions for yourself*

then check out the "Coach's Challenge" in the next chapter of this book.

Be challenged; aspire to make a positive difference!
– Coach John S. Nagy

E. The Coach's Challenge!

Here are some of those key questions referred to in the previous chapter. They appear simple and are tougher then they might first appear. People on the "success-track" will confront them, answer them in-depth and willingly share them with a coach.

You can work through this much more easily if you can envision yourself as if you are in the future, three years from now. Answer these questions as if you're looking back over the last 3 years:

1. **Future Vision:** Effective choices come from knowing what you want to accomplish.

   ☐ What did the next level of success (from where you are now) look and feel like for you? Express your answers to this question as actions that you see yourself as having taken during the past three years.

2. **Future Conditions:** Measurement tells us how much we won.

   ☐ How did you know that you had achieved this level?

   ☐ What were the telltale signs?

3. **Future Results:** Motivation fuels our actions.

   ☐ What would being at this level mean for you professionally and personally?

   ☐ How would that feel? (Name the emotions.)

Now, come back to the present.

4. Roadblocks: Sabotage prevents success. It is defined as actions and choices that hinder or block forward movement.

- ❐ What personal sabotage, if any, has prevented you from getting to the next level?

- ❐ What have you done professionally and personally in the past to deal with this?

5. Traveling Fuel: We get there by choice and personal investment.

- ❐ How motivated are you to achieve this next level? (Challenge: express this as action.)

- ❐ What are you willing to invest?

- ❐ What are you willing to give up?

Now, work up a plan.

6. Start Time: Start times are more necessary than Deadlines – they lessen stress and get projects moving as they should.

- ❐ How soon – exactly – should you achieve this next level if you allow nothing to stop your progress?

- ❐ When should you start taking action to assure a less stressful success? (Your start time is based on your deadline and includes the amount of time you need to complete the task(s) with plenty of time for review, corrections and adjustments)

7. First Steps: Strong success is a forged chain of choices, actions and events. What actions must you take first to start the process going so you can achieve your goal on schedule?

Now, make sure you know you're winning.

8. Path Support: Effective efforts occur when you actively engage principles, rules, policies, guidelines, people, situations, tools and materials that are supportive to your efforts. What structure, if put in place now, will guarantee your success?

9. Tracking: Holding yourself accountable is tricky when you're both the rule- maker and the rule enforcer.

- ❐ What are your ideas regarding accountability?

- ❐ What does accountability mean for you, specifically?

- ❐ What type of accountability works best for you?

- ❐ How do you hold and keep yourself accountable?

10. Outside Leverage: Having outside perspective keeps us honest and this requires our continuous authorization of the outside perspective to give us honest feedback.

- ❐ Whom are you going to empower to help you hold yourself accountable?

- ❐ How will you empower them to help you hold yourself accountable?

(What's next? How about sharing your responses with your coach!)

F. A Simple & Honest Business Plan: Questions

Here are some questions you can use to help you as you formulate your business plan:

Inside-Out View, with Focus on Being and Doing: Ask:

1. Who are you? (Not *you* personally but who you are in business.)
2. What do you do? (or what *will* you do?)
3. What is your (intended) business?
4. What are your (intended) products or services?
5. What are the benefits your clients will receive when they buy from you or invest in you?
6. Where are you working location-wise?
7. What are your hours?

Outside In View, with Focus on Your Target: Ask:

1. Who is your target? (Ultimately, whom are you trying to reach and serve?)
2. What specifically is (are) your market(s)?
3. Where do your potential clients usually play?
4. What are their usual habits and tendencies?
5. What is their pain?
6. How does your service help them?
7. Where will they be serviced?
8. How will they be serviced?

Connections, with Focus on Getting Attention: Ask:

1. How are your future clients best reached?
2. What effective methods will you use to reach them?
3. What have you seen others using and how did it work for them?
4. What support will you need?
5. Whom do you know who can help you in these efforts?
6. What unusual method, if done right, might get good results too?
7. What percentage of your budget will be used for these methods?

Budget, with Focus on Your Expense Flow: Ask:

1. What personal net income stream do you need now and want to see created for yourself within one year? (You may want to create a personal expense sheet to get a realistic idea as to the best and worse case situations. Be honest here! If you do not know what your costs are personally, you may run into problems later that will interfere with your business.)
2. What would that be in gross dollar terms? (Factor in taxes and deductions.)
3. What do you anticipate to be the total yearly expenses based on your understanding of the business you will be operating? (Include all related materials, services, utilities, salaries, etc. that are typical for a business such as yours.)
4. What would all of this look like in terms of monthly, quarterly and yearly flow? (Create a time-line that shows the cash that will be required and received during each period, indicating deadlines as to when each flow/expense will occur.)
5. How many personal expenses are actually supportive business expenses?

Profit, with Focus on Your ROI (Return on Investment): Ask:

1. How many income streams are you involved in?
2. What is your ROI for each income stream you are working?
3. What are the projected "absolute best possible results" you could expect for the year from each income stream? Include the probabilities in hard numbers even if assumed.
4. What are the projected "absolute minimum acceptable results" you would accept for the year? Include the probabilities in hard numbers even if assumed.

Future, with Focus on Your FIVE-YEAR projection: Ask:

1. In five years, where do you want to be? (Please describe your vision and situation.)
2. In five years, what are you doing?
3. In five years, what have you achieved?
4. In five years, what opportunities do you see opening up for you?

Executive Summary, with Focus on Your Overview: Now, put it all together.

1. Create a cover page with all the elements clearly bulleted.
2. Keep it to one page and put yourself in "minimum verbosity mode."

Have an uncommonly bodacious success in your business and your life! – Coach John Nagy

G. About Coach John S. Nagy

Coach John S. Nagy is a multi-degree Professional Business and Life Coach and Technical Advisor who provides coaching support to business and career professionals throughout the world; his offices are located in the Tampa Bay area. He has run his own coaching practice since January 1989.

His corporation, "Coaching for Success, Inc.," operates on the same principles he asks his clients to practice. Coach Nagy started his organization with a rich background in the business development, project management, and consulting fields. He specializes in systems evaluation and development, along with keeping people in action once a goal is clearly identified and committed to.

Coach Nagy has a *Bachelors of Science in* Electrical Engineering and a Masters of Science in Engineering Management, both from the University of South Florida. He is also a *graduate of Coach U.* He helped spearhead the formation of the International Coaching Federation (ICF) in 1996, was *ICF's First Executive Director*, and was the *founder and first host* of *The Tampa Bay Area Coaching Association* at that time.

Coach Nagy is a well-recognized, state-certified mediator in Florida, with over a decade of experience. He mediates court-ordered cases in the 13th Judicial Circuit of Hillsborough County and trains fellow mediators throughout the state.

John is also a columnist and published author since the early 1990's. He writes, speaks and trains others extensively on a wide variety of subjects related to personal, professional and business development – *all from a coaching prospective*.

Coach Nagy and his wife Candy, along with their two sons, reside in the South-Central area of Pasco County, Florida. (His sons want you to know that their dad also coaches their soccer team.)